MW01075800

MARTIN OF TOURS

RÉGINE PERNOUD

MARTIN OF TOURS

Soldier, Bishop, and Saint

Translated by
Michael J. Miller

IGNATIUS PRESS   SAN FRANCISCO

Cover art:
Saint Martin and the Beggar
Pordenone (1483–1576)
S. Rocco, Venice, Italy
© Cameraphoto Arte, Venice / Art Resource, New York

Cover design by Roxanne Mei Lum

For those men and women who,
following the example of Saint Martin,
will have to develop a new form of culture
for the third millennium:
Fanny and Julie,
Gregory and Clement,
Helen
and the others . . .

CONTENTS

ACKNOWLEDGMENTS

All quotations from the writings of Sulpicius Severus are taken from *The Western Fathers: Being the Lives of SS. Martin of Tours, Ambrose, Augustine of Hippo, Honoratus of Arles and Germanus of Auxerre*, translated by F. R. Hoare (New York: Sheed & Ward, 1954). Reprinted by kind permission of Sheed & Ward (U.K.), an imprint of the Continuum International Publishing Group.

The translator has used brackets to indicate words that were added for clarification or that otherwise differed from the text of Régine Pernoud's book.

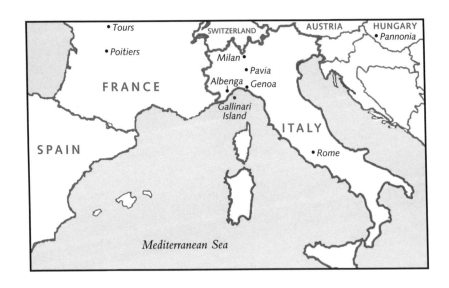

PROLOGUE

November 11 is now a red-letter day on the French civil calendar: in 1918 that date marked the end of the slaughter that was the First World War. But even before France was called France, that date, the eleventh of November, had been a date on the calendar used throughout Christendom because it commemorated the burial at Tours of the amazing individual whom we call Saint Martin.

He was an amazing and even a paradoxical man: he never accomplished what he had hoped to do, and yet his accomplishments surpassed all possible expectations. To begin with, this man, who had always tried to go unnoticed, enjoyed extraordinary popularity. He wanted to be a hermit, to flee the world and devote himself to ascetical practices; instead he was constantly surrounded by people, during his lifetime and after his death: the pilgrimage shrine of Saint Martin in Tours was once the most important after the three great pilgrimage sites of Christianity, Jerusalem, Rome, and, later on, Saint James of Compostela. He is remembered as a soldier, and indeed he was one, albeit entirely against his will. He had refused to be ordained a priest, considering himself unworthy, and yet he became a bishop. He had fled the world and sought a life of seclusion, but instead his biography was written while he was still living!

Thanks to those who discerned the extraordinary qualities in this rather reticent, unassuming man who resolutely practiced poverty, we know the story of his life. It spans the fourth century, in which the Church became free at last to live above ground, only to be torn by dissension so wide-spread that it almost brought her to ruin.

There are not many individuals whose biographies were written during the fourth century, especially during their lifetime. This was the case, however, with Martin of Tours, thanks to his friend Sulpicius Severus, who survived him long enough to record for us also the story of his death. And so we have the unusual good fortune of possessing a contemporary document to tell us about a man who, throughout his life, sought only to live among his peers, in obscurity.

In Search of Holiness

Sulpicius Severus was handsome, young, and rich. He lived in Bordeaux, a particularly prosperous town in the fourth century, where he received an outstanding education; he practiced law there and excelled in his profession because of his great eloquence. His family belonged to that Gallo-Roman aristocracy which enjoyed the favor of the Roman emperors because their power depended upon it. Thus, in the region that would later be called Aquitaine, there were several families that owned enormous estates and a large number of slaves and were extremely wealthy. The province was crossed by navigable waterways, which guaranteed abundant commerce. Bordeaux at that time had the reputation of being an "intellectual" city; like Toulouse, it had quite a number of citizens who had conformed completely to the customs and tastes characteristic of the Roman Empire. In the region surrounding Toulouse archeologists have found as many busts and sculptures from the imperial era as they have in the vicinity of Rome—artwork intended to ornament the villas where these opulent families lived.

Sulpicius Severus, being a lawyer, had made a name for

himself in "upper-middle-class" circles while he was still a very young man. His reputation is inseparable from that of the man who would later be called Paulinus of Nola, with whom he was bound by ties of friendship. Paulinus, a lawyer like Sulpicius, came from an even richer family than his and was likewise an avid man of letters. It is easy to imagine the two friends going together to the thermal baths or attending the literary gatherings of the day, where people discussed the poetry of Virgil or Ovid, or perhaps the eloquence of Cicero. Paulinus, who was highly valued by Emperor Valentinian II, had been appointed for a time as governor of Campania, but he had resigned from his official duties and returned to Bordeaux so as to lead there a life of elegant leisure, as was the fashion then on the banks of the Garonne River.

Now a new factor came into his life around the year 389 (Paulinus was about thirty-six years old at the time): he was touched by the gospel. The Christian religion, which had been spreading freely for a good sixty years—the Edict of Milan promulgated by Constantine, which ended the persecutions, dated back to the year 313—would thoroughly transform that pleasure-seeking aristocrat. In the year 390, together with his wife, Therasia, he received baptism. His encounter with the Christian faith may have been fostered by the great sorrow he had experienced at the death of a beloved brother.

Soon afterward, Sulpicius in turn was touched by grace. He had been married only a little while, and perhaps his mother-in-law, Bassula, who was a fervent Christian, had had some influence upon him. He received baptism, but his wife died shortly after, and he found himself disowned by his father, who could not abide his conversion. Moreover, Sulpicius himself was preparing to follow the example of his friend Paulinus, who had begun to divest himself of all his property, following the evangelical counsel of poverty to the letter. Of what he inherited from his wife, Sulpicius kept only a small lot, a kind of temporary lodging, where from then on he would welcome a number of other Christian converts who wished to lead a life of prayer and asceticism. The place was called Primuliacum in Latin, and it has been identified with the little city of Alzonne on the road from Toulouse to Carcassonne, not far from Bram, in the Aude in Languedoc. Sulpicius must have taken up residence there in 394 or a little earlier.

It was there, too, that he received the letters that Paulinus wrote to him. For example, the one in which he expresses, in the rather emphatic language of that era, his admiration for his young friend:

> But you, my most beloved brother, were converted to the Lord by a greater miracle [than I]. For you were closer to your prime, you were winning greater eulogies, the burden of your inheritance was lighter, yet you were no poorer in store of wealth; you were still prominent in the fame of the forum which is the theatre of the world, and you held the palm for glory of eloquence. Yet with a sudden urge you shook off the slavish yoke of sin, and broke the deadly bonds of flesh and blood. Neither the additional riches brought by your marriage into a consular household nor the easy tendency to sin after your marriage [i.e., after he was widowed] which followed your celibate youth could draw you back from the narrow entrance to salvation, from the steep path of virtue to the soft, broad road trodden by many.[1]

And Paulinus continues, recalling the friendship that united them in their youth:

> *What shall I render to the Lord for* this grace in addition to *all his bounty to me?* (Ps 115[116]:12). For through this grace He has

[1] Ancient Christian Writers Series, *Letters of St. Paulinus of Nola*, trans. and annot. by P. G. Walsh, vol. 1 and 2 (Westminster, Md.: The Newman Press, 1966–1967). The citation is from vol. 1, Letter 5, par. 5, pp. 56–57.

joined you to me not only as a most beloved friend in our earlier life in the world, but also as an inseparable companion and partner in the spiritual brotherhood of His affairs. . . . [T]hat intimate friendship of our earlier life, when we still loved the things which we now reject in Christ, marked us out for each other in the love of Christ.[2]

Paulinus had returned with his wife to Campania, where he settled at Nola, a little town founded of old by Saint Felix, who was buried there. From then on Paulinus and his wife led a very austere life, dwelling in the same house but living as brother and sister, and devoting themselves to the needs of the pilgrims and the poor. Paulinus had already been ordained a priest in Barcelona, and in 409 he was appointed bishop of Nola. In another one of his letters to Sulpicius he writes: "You revealed the increase of your inheritance amongst the saints. This you did by your wholesome disposal of the burdens of this world, for you have purchased heaven and Christ at the price of brittle worldly goods."[3] Thus the correspondence between the two friends leaves no doubt as to their complete conversion, which led both of them to give away their fortunes. It is said that even Sulpicius, who retained his ownership of Primuliacum, only did so in order to host friends there, as well as his mother-in-law, with whom he maintained close ties of friendship and whose fervent faith was evident. He experienced scruples, however, on that account, and Paulinus reassured him:

And why should you lament that you on the contrary are still unhappily clinging to the slimy dregs of hell below, just because from your letter you appear not to have sold one petty estate? Your forfeiture of your present right even to that farm is equivalent to selling it, so that by the greater fruits of your

[2] Ibid., vol. 1, Letter 11, par. 1, 5, pp. 90, 93.
[3] Ibid., vol. 1, Letter 1, par. 1, pp. 29–30.

faith you showed to God a twofold dedication . . . for the goods you have kept back are possessed by the church which you serve.[4]

Sulpicius Severus, while in retirement on his estate, received many visitors, and that is how he heard about the bishop of Tours, Martin.

As for Paulinus, even before his conversion he had been in contact with Martin. Later on Sulpicius would tell of the circumstances. "A man named Paulinus, who was afterwards to be an example to all, had begun to suffer from acute pain in one eye and a fairly thick film had by now grown over the pupil. Martin, by touching the eye with a fine paintbrush, restored it to its former state and at the same time banished all the pain."[5] This probably took place during a journey that Martin made to Vienne, and it is conjectured that the two friends must have had an ongoing discussion about this cure.

But this was certainly not the only reason that prompted Sulpicius to go to see Martin. Plainly, the reputation of the bishop of Tours had aroused his curiosity even before that. "I had previously heard accounts of his faith, his life, and his powers and burned with the desire to know the man himself", he writes. "I therefore undertook as a labor of love a pilgrimage to see him." Indeed, in those days the journey from the regions along the Garonne River to the banks of the Loire River was long. Traveling from north to south was easy through the Saône and Rhône valleys, but that was not the case in the western territories that drain into the Atlantic

[4] Ibid., vol. 1, Letter 24, par. 1, p. 51.

[5] As indicated in the Acknowledgments, all quotations from the writings of Sulpicius Severus are quoted from the translation by F. R. Hoare, in *The Western Fathers: Being the Lives of SS. Martin of Tours, Ambrose, Augustine of Hippo, Honoratus of Arles and Germanus of Auxerre* (New York: Sheed & Ward, 1954). Reprinted by kind permission of Sheed & Ward (U.K.), an imprint of the Continuum International Publishing Group.—TRANS.

Ocean; furthermore, the Roman roads crossed France from east to west.

"At the same time," Sulpicius relates, "I was all on fire to write his life." His natural talents would find expression in a literary work that was perfectly suited to his deep feelings. He decided, therefore, to make the journey. "You would never credit the humility and kindness with which [Martin] received me on that occasion. He congratulated himself and praised the Lord because I had thought so highly of him that I had undertaken a long journey especially to see him." And he tells of his embarrassment when Martin invited him to share in a meal, and "it was he who fetched the water for me to wash my hands and, in the evening, it was he who washed my feet. Nor had I the courage to remonstrate or resist. I was so overcome by his authority that I would have felt it impious to do anything but acquiesce."

No doubt this visit made a profound impression on Sulpicius. He found in Martin just as saintly an individual as he had been said to be. "But all his talk while I was there was of the necessity of renouncing the allurements of the world and the burdens of secular life in order to follow the Lord Jesus freely and unimpeded." And the following lines suggest even more the extent to which the conversations with Martin must have affected his guest: indeed, Martin held up Paulinus to him as an example! "He quoted as an outstanding example in our own day the case of his Excellency Paulinus, whom I mentioned earlier. He had abandoned immense wealth to follow Christ and was almost alone in our times in fulfilling the evangelical counsels. 'There,' Martin kept exclaiming, 'there is someone for you to follow.'" We can surmise that his words elicited an emotional response from his interlocutor! Martin drew from the decision of Paulinus a lesson for his generation: "For a rich man with great possessions, by selling all and giving to the poor, had illustrated Our Lord's saying, that what is impossible to do is in fact a possibility."

After that memorable encounter, Sulpicius was able to undertake what would be the great accomplishment of his life: writing the life of Martin of Tours. It took nothing less than the call of the gospel and the power of the faith to draw together two men who were so dissimilar, from such different social backgrounds.

I

Martin's Childhood and Youth

It was in the year 316, or perhaps 317, that a little boy came into the world to whom the name Martin was given, which is the diminutive form of Mars, the god of war. This took place in Pannonia, in the village of Sabaria—no doubt the town that today is called Szombathely, not far from Lake Balaton in modern-day Hungary.

We might reflect on the date of his birth: recall that only three or four years earlier, precisely at the beginning of the year 313, Emperor Constantine had declared the Christian Church free by the famous Edict of Milan. He abolished the harsh measures taken against its adherents by the previous emperors, in particular Diocletian, who had not abdicated until A.D. 305, yielding the throne to other heads of state who were just as implacably opposed to the religion of the Christ. With the reign of Constantine, a period of living in the daylight commenced, following the more or less totally underground activity of the preceding centuries.

There was a reason why Martin was named "little Mars" by his parents: he was the first and would remain the only child of a soldier who had risen from the ranks. The father had been made a military tribune and obviously hoped that his son would follow in his footsteps and be a soldier as well.

That is why he gave him the name, which was destined to become so widespread—in social settings quite different from the military! Even today, in France, there are two to three times as many Martins as Duponts; we will return to this subject later on.

The family did not stay long in Pannonia. A few years after Martin's birth, his father was declared a veteran, and the army allotted to him a house with a piece of ground where he could spend his retirement. It was located in the plain of the Po River, in Ticinum, a place that today we call Pavia, a peaceful city on the banks of the Ticino River [in Switzerland it flows into the Po], one day's journey on foot from Milan. That is where Martin would pass his childhood. It was a childhood like any other, about which we know very little. It was most probably spent between family and school, though, since at that time schools brought children together almost everywhere in the immense territory ruled by the Romans.

For Rome was indeed in that era "a city that has a country", even several countries. It covered all of Europe (except Germany), north Africa, and Asia Minor. Over this immense territory reigned the emperor or, rather, the emperors, since it had been decided at the beginning of the fourth century that four sovereigns would divide up the empire. As of the year 324, Constantine would again become the sole ruler, and subsequently it came about that many individuals would lay claim to the empire, most of them officers elected by their armies. The army was the principal means of maintaining the empire. Rome ruled through its military forces, and also through its officials: a rather meddlesome administration, which made the power of the state felt everywhere and raised taxes for it.

Martin's family was part of this privileged institution, the army; they seemed to have been perfectly assimilated into that vast collective enterprise that dominated Europe then, and they spent peaceful days in Ticinum. There was, however, one incident: when Martin was ten years old, he ran away. For forty-eight hours he was missing, and his worried parents looked everywhere for him. On the third day Martin reappeared, in perfect health and quite calm. Yet he did not answer the questions of his family and friends but kept absolutely silent about those two days spent away from home. Only much later would they learn the reason for his flight. Martin went into a church, probably in Ticinum itself; he lived there for two days asking questions and demanding answers; he even wanted to get ready for baptism, which would have required a much longer time of preparation. Therefore he was compelled to go back home, after having someone make the Sign of the Cross over him, as was the custom among Christians.

His parents would know nothing about it. For their part, they observed the common religious practices, adored Jupiter, Mars, Minerva, and the others, and offered sacrifices to those gods according to custom. Above all, they revered the emperor himself as a god, went down on bended knee before him or before his statue, and burned incense to him on the prescribed days.

But another light had dawned on Martin—due to the influence of a playmate, friend, or fellow student? No one knows. Something made him want to learn more about those Christians, many of whom had been tortured and had died during the times of persecution that were still so recent. In the church at Pavia he heard people sing the glory of these martyrs. And they were also fond of talking about those who, in Egypt or Syria or other places, offered the rest of their lives for another sort of martyrdom they inflicted upon themselves through ascetic practices. Martin became ardent with admiration at the thought of these men who withdrew to the desert and passed their time in prayer, living on locusts and wild honey like Saint John the Baptist in olden times, of whom he probably had also heard them speak.

For a twelve-year-old to dream about living in the desert may seem surprising. But we have to imagine ourselves in Martin's day, in that milieu in Pavia where he most likely had been able to meet a certain number of Christians among his companions and schoolmates. The Christian community there, no doubt, was quite large. In the following centuries, and notably in the seventh century, Pavia would play an important role from the religious and cultural perspective: this was the town where Paul the Deacon would be instructed, who was destined to be very influential in the court of Charlemagne. Martin felt drawn to this community, since it was in order to join them that he had run away without his parents' knowledge.

Now conversations among the Christians, during Martin's youth, were affected by the complete change of atmosphere that had come about. A few decades before, those same Christian communities had lived underground in silence and had marveled at their martyred brethren. The reign of Diocletian had provided plenty of stories of tortures courageously endured, painful deaths bravely undergone—everything that would one day become part of the *Golden Legend*, with the indispensable embellishments, was at that time an almost everyday reality. And then suddenly a new, astonishing reality opened up for the followers of Christ: the emperor himself granted to their religion—which yesterday had been persecuted—his protection, giving rise to all sorts of hopes and opportunities. Would he not then establish the Kingdom of God upon earth himself? That was the question that

Christians asked from then on, and among the news reports that made the rounds there was mention of those hermits, who soon won the admiration of the crowds. The movement was just beginning, but already people were talking about men in Egypt who were leaving the towns to live in the wilderness, a Pachomius, an Anthony, whose names were pronounced with reverence by the members of the Christian communities. That explains Martin's quest, which was probably inspired by the stories that circulated then by word of mouth.

Meanwhile he spent his adolescence in an exemplary way, living with his parents, who shared neither his enthusiasm nor his hopes. One day there was a rude awakening: in the year 331 the emperor issued an edict requiring all the sons of veterans to enlist in the Roman army. Martin was fifteen years old, the age for enlisting, and he was the son of a veteran, so he had to join the army.

This was the first of the many vicissitudes that would stubbornly repeat themselves for as long as he lived. Martin would never be able to act as he intended; he could never decide for himself on his destiny. To start with, this decree radically put an end to all his dreams of the desert and the life of a hermit. "As a prisoner in chains, he bound himself by the military oath", writes Sulpicius Severus. This suggests that he did not willingly accept the imperial decree—far from it! If there was one state in life that he had never dreamed of, it was certainly that of the soldier. And yet that is what he was being constrained to become.

His father must have had something to do with it: that former military tribune, now a veteran, had no intention of letting his son avoid the life that he himself had led, in which he had prominently distinguished himself. He was the one who handed Martin over to the soldiers who came to notify him of his conscription. Shackled, then, and uttering futile protests, he went off to begin military life.

The Roman Empire during that era always gave the impression of being invulnerable. It had even provided itself recently with a prestigious capital, the "new Rome", to which the people would soon give the name of Constantinople. Built in six years by manpower consisting of an enormous number of slaves and requisitioned Goths—with thick walls, superb dwellings along the two principal arteries, temples, statues, fountains, a seaport with stone piers—the city was inaugurated in the year 330. There, Constantine was to finish his days in 337. Martin and his fellow enlistees must have heard about it; it was the marvel of the world, from the heart of the empire to the remotest frontiers.

It did nothing, however, to dispel one source of uneasiness on the frontiers: those "barbarians" who had already invaded around fifty years previously, in 276 and 277, advancing to the outskirts of Rome and venturing into Gaul, as far as Autun in Burgundy. The Goths, the Alamanni, and the Franks were becoming a threat again. More than ever, the empire needed its army.

And the boy who had dreamed of becoming a hermit in the desert, so as to spend his life in prayer, was going to be a soldier—a soldier in the Roman army, which made little allowance for dreaming, much less for prayer. He would even be assigned to the *scholae imperatoris*, that is, to the imperial guard, which suggests that he must have been solid, muscular, well-built. The imperial guard consisted of around five hundred magnificently outfitted cavalrymen, who were responsible for defending the emperor whenever he went on a military campaign. His father must have been proud of him: his son seemed to be assured of a brilliant career, at the heart of the Roman army in which he himself had fought his whole life long. He was certainly pleased to learn that the imperial guard would be stationed at Amiens, a city in Gaul near the frontier. There Martin would spend the greater part of his stint as a soldier, drilling daily to the sound of the trumpet, taking care of his gear and his horse, maintaining public order by patrolling back and forth, and from time to time dutifully escorting some exalted personage.

Perhaps the father would not have been reassured by the rumors and occasional sarcastic remarks that went around concerning his son. Didn't his fellow guardsmen tell stories about the rather surprising way that Martin treated his slave? Instead of letting himself be served, he was the one who served when they took their meals together; what's more, he would go so far as to clean the slave's sandals! This fueled the jesting, as did Martin's conduct on other occasions, since he did not try to show off in front of women and never spent the nights carousing when on holiday. Yet he proved to be an irreproachable comrade-in-arms, always ready to serve, and so the other guards were content to laugh at his strange behavior, without taunting him any more about it.

At the beginning of the fourth century, slavery was still in force. The institution was basic to society in antiquity, which was divided categorically into two parts: the class of free men, who went to the forum, took part in discussions about politics and sometimes in literary gatherings as well, and who found it natural to leave all the manual work to the other part of society, the slaves. The latter, in general, were prisoners of war, sometimes the children of slaves, but that was uncommon, because slaves had no right to a family or to marriage. Indeed, they had no right to anything characteristic of a human being; in antiquity, a slave was something that one bought and sold, that in no way could be the subject of personal rights. We have it on the authority of Aristotle, who calmly declares that "the usefulness of slaves is about the same as that of domestic animals." It is evident that the gospel proved to be incompatible with slavery, and that Saint Paul expressed a view diametrically opposed to it: "There is neither Jew nor Greek, there is neither slave nor free, there is neither male nor female, for you are all one in Christ Jesus" (Gal 3:28). One of Saint Paul's letters, the one written to Philemon, specifies what action is to be taken with regard to the slavery that was so deeply rooted in the customs of the day: Paul sends the slave Onesimus back to his owner, to whom he is writing, and begs him to welcome him "no longer as a slave but more than a slave, as a beloved brother" (Philem 16).

It was in fact as a brother that Martin was treating his own slave, and this implies that, during his childhood in Pavia, he must have met a certain number of Christians and remembered what he had learned from them. Furthermore, it was in his day, with the liberty granted to the Church, that the first measures would be taken against slavery. "For the Church, there is neither freeman nor slave", Bishop John Chrysostom would say. Then again, the Christians used to recount the sufferings endured by certain slaves during the persecutions, whose courage they greatly admired—a Saint Blandina or a Saint Felicity. As a result, in Martin's own day, Emperor Constantine (the first) had mitigated somewhat the lot of the slave, among other things forbidding the separation of families. With the beginning of the century, in the year 305, the ecclesiastical councils—beginning with that of Elvira in Spain—imposed seven years of penance upon any master who killed his slave. Subsequently these councils would multiply their decrees to defend the emancipated or to guarantee fugitive slaves the right of asylum in the churches. In other words, to the rest of fourth-century society, the Christians appeared to be troublemakers: it was so convenient to resort to slavery for all the laborious or unpleasant work in life, and, what is more, it was free!

The fact remains that Martin treated his slave like a brother and that this conduct heralded a new age, a complete break with the societies of antiquity. "Topsy-turvy fashion, it was the master who performed the services, often to the extent of taking off the servant's boots himself and cleaning them. They took their meals together and it was generally the master who waited." Martin may have been a soldier, as his father wanted and the law decreed, but he was by no means a soldier like the others, and this makes more comprehensible the gesture that would immortalize him.

It happened in Amiens, at one of the city gates, in the year 335, during an extremely harsh winter. "Many were dying of the intense cold." A poor man was there, half-naked, shivering, asking for alms; no one was paying any attention to him. As for Martin, he had nothing to give him; under the splendid uniform of the imperial guard, he had neither silver nor copper coins. What should he do? Pass him by as everyone else was doing? Martin took his sword, "cut the cape in two and gave one half to the beggar, putting on the rest himself again". His biographer adds that the bystanders laughed at the spectacle, "for he looked grotesque in the mutilated garment". The white *chlamys* or cape was the uniform of that elite guard which served the emperor, the members of which were called *candidati*, which means "men clothed in white". It was a cloak with a slit, fastened at the right shoulder with a brooch; the upper part of it was lined with lambskin, and perhaps it was that lined part that Martin cut off with his sword to give to the beggar. At any rate, he could not have suspected the importance his action would acquire over the centuries, as it was depicted in so many frescoes, paintings,

sculptures, and manuscript illuminations. As long as the
Church endures, Martin will thus cut his cloak in two so as to
give half of it to the poor man.

The episode is well known. "That night, in his sleep, Martin saw Christ wearing the half of his cape with which he had
clothed the beggar." He was invited to look very carefully at
the Lord and to recognize the garment he had donated. Then
he heard Jesus say in a loud voice to the host of angels that
surrounded them: "Martin is still only a catechumen but he
has clothed Me with this garment."

This vision sanctioned and hallowed in a way Martin's
deed and was a milestone in his personal development. He
was not yet baptized, but he knew the gospel: this sense of
sharing with which he was imbued meant that he had assimilated the evangelical precepts into his interior life from his
youth: clothing the naked. And the vision itself revealed to
him what the Gospel assures us is true: "As you did it to one
of the least of these my brethren, you did it to me" (Mt
25:40). His attraction to the Christian faith, which characterized him from his childhood, was not just a reverie; as of that
moment, he had assimilated the essential message. And yet he
was still only a catechumen. No doubt, though, such a vision
would expedite his preparations for baptism.

Historians are uncertain as to when he received the sacrament. We prefer to follow the chronology established by
Jacques Fontaine, who has studied in minute detail the biography of Saint Martin written by Sulpicius Severus: he gives
the year 335 as the date for both the act of charity and
Martin's baptism. Therefore he would have been eighteen
years old at the time.

It is at that moment, moreover, that the chronological
difficulties begin. The biography relates that Martin would
have liked to leave the army immediately, but that he re-

mained at the request of one of his friends, a military tribune, who wanted to complete the time of his enlistment and then renounce the world also, in order to consecrate himself entirely to God. "Buoyed up by this hope, Martin remained a soldier, though only in name, for nearly two years after his baptism." And here we find the principal question mark that historians have stumbled on: Must we conclude that he left the service two years after his baptism, or rather assume that he completed his time, the normal period of enlistment for a soldier? The two years that Sulpicius Severus allows are in fact not nearly enough to bring the account to the time when he would leave, that is, during his encounter with Caesar Julian (the one who has gone down in history as Julian the Apostate), and the ensuing challenge. Jacques Fontaine thinks that the biographer was somewhat embarrassed about referring to the long stint in the army, since Martin's departure would not take place until 356.

Here we come upon a question that, after all is said and done, unceasingly confronts the Christian conscience, and that we find even today across a broad spectrum of intellectual groups: the relation between the Christian and war. Military life, quite obviously, exposes him to the risk of shedding blood; it is contrary, therefore, not only to the precepts of the Old Testament—"Thou shalt not kill"—but also to those of the gospel concerning love of neighbor. Several soldiers appear in the Gospels, chief among them being the centurion, at whose faith Christ himself marveled, so that even in our day, at every Mass just before Communion, his words are repeated: "Lord, I am not worthy to have you come under my roof; but only say the word, and my servant will be healed" (Mt 8:8). The Lord could have asked him to abandon his profession before he would respond to his request and heal the sick man, but, given the centurion's act of faith, he made no such stipulation. In that instance, we might note, he proved to be much less demanding than some fiercely conscientious objectors nowadays.

Suffice it to say that this immensely complicated problem is still with us, and that in the early centuries of the Church it gave rise to many a vocation to martyrdom. In Martin's own day, the Council of Arles (314) explicitly emphasized that Christians did not have to abandon the military after their baptism. We should note here that, even though there has never been any question of a "holy war" in the Christian world—as opposed to the world of Islam, which views *jihad* as a means approved by Muhammad for propagating his faith—the Church has nevertheless admitted, albeit with difficulty and reservations, the possibility or even the necessity of a "just war". Over the course of time this notion has been defined more precisely in the Christian mind with the principles of legitimate defense and war of liberation.

The fact remains that, as far as Martin and Sulpicius Severus are concerned, a baptized Christian can go into battle only with repugnance at having to shed blood "professionally". The episode that furnished Martin with the occasion for leaving the army will demonstrate this clearly. Many accounts of the lives of the saints from that era relate the martyrdom of Christian soldiers who rebelled against an impious caesar and who preferred to undergo torments rather than continue to serve—for example, Saints Victor, Nabor, and Felix. Among Martin's contemporaries, two officers of the imperial guard, Juventinus and Maximinus, were to be put to death by Julian the Apostate; the emperor had ordered them to offer incense to him, which amounted to treating him as a god, and they had refused.

As a result of the painstaking investigations of Jacques Fontaine, we can follow his opinion and believe that Martin completed the prescribed time of service as a soldier: twenty-five years—it being understood that during that time he was not obliged to shed blood. As a member of the imperial guard he belonged to a group of noncombatants, "ensuring public order, the protection of the imperial post, the transfer of prisoners or the safety of dignitaries". As a mounted imperial guardsman, Martin would have found a way, as many other Christians had before him, of "satisfying the requirements of their faith, while fulfilling their temporal duties".[1]

Whatever the case may be, this period would have a striking conclusion. From 352 on, the barbarians began again to threaten the northern frontiers of the empire; they seized several localities, for instance, Broutages (modern-day Brumath), and threatened Mainz and Worms, the city of the Vangiones. Caesar Julian immediately went to Alsace and beyond the Rhine. His imperial guard joined up with him precisely in the territory of the Vangiones, at Worms, which was under siege by the enemy. The members of the guard were called together by Julian to receive the bonus that was usually paid on the eve of combat, which in Latin was called the *donativum*—a sort of gratuity meant to encourage them. This was already a long-standing custom: a scene in which the *donativum* is being distributed was depicted in the second-century bas-reliefs on the column of Trajan in Rome. Now this would be Martin's chance to confront the caesar directly.

We will let Sulpicius Severus relate the incident:

Meanwhile the barbarians were making incursions into Gaul and the Caesar Julian concentrated his army at Worms. There he began to distribute a bonus to the soldiers. They were called up one by one in the usual way until Martin's turn came. But he thought it would be a suitable time for applying

[1] Jacques Fontaine, *Vie de saint Martin* [Life of Saint Martin] (Cerf, collection Sources Chrétiennes, no. 133, 1967), vol. 2, p. 506.

for his discharge, for he did not think that it would be honest for him to take the bonus if he was not going to fight. So he said to the Caesar: "I have been your soldier up to now. Let me now be God's. Let someone who is going to fight have your bonus. I am Christ's soldier; I am not allowed to fight."

These words put the tyrant into a rage and he said that it was from fear of the battle that was to be fought the next day that he wanted to quit the service, not from religious motives. But Martin was undaunted; in fact he stood all the firmer when they tried to frighten him.

"If it is put down to cowardice," he said, "and not to faith, I will stand unarmed in front of the battle-line tomorrow and I will go unscathed through the enemy's columns in the name of the Lord Jesus, protected by the sign of the Cross instead of by shield and helmet."

It was a dramatic scene, and the emperor took him at his word; he ordered Martin to be thrown into prison until the next day. We may suppose that he spent the night in prayer. Then, in the morning, the Germanic invaders "sent envoys to ask for peace, surrendering themselves and all they had". It has been said, consequently, that Martin's only "military exploit" ended in victory!

After this unexpected episode, Martin in fact left the army. It would not be the only occasion in his life when the Sign of the Cross would become for him a sign of victory.

2

Martin and Hilary of Poitiers

The year is 356. Martin has been relieved of his military duties and is free at last to lead the sort of life to which he is drawn. No doubt he will hasten to begin the life of a hermit, which was the object of his adolescent hopes. Will he head for Egypt? Syria? That is where the monks live who have made a name for themselves, like Anthony, that master of the spiritual life, who died in that same year, 356, and whose biography would be written by Bishop Athanasius. Or else like Pachomius, who was surrounded by young men whom he trained to read the Bible. We can imagine Martin being impatient to take charge of his own destiny now and set out on the path he has always desired to follow.

He probably went to Trier, where the Christian community was quite active. No doubt it was there that he heard about someone who would play a decisive role in his career: Hilary of Poitiers. Trier at that time was a capital. The city, located on the banks of the Moselle River, could claim the honor of being the most ancient city in Germany, and since the end of the second century it had been the principal residence of the emperors. Constantine had settled there with his mother, Helena; he commissioned the building of new ramparts, of which the world-renowned *Porta nigra* still stands today. The city would continue to be the imperial residence until the end of the fourth century. It was, moreover, a transportation hub, and its river port was commercially significant. It is likely that Martin had stayed there occasionally even as a soldier; another reason is that the bishop of Trier, Maximinus, had a reputation for saintliness, which would be confirmed shortly after his death. Much later, in the time of Charlemagne, his tomb would become the site of an enormous Benedictine abbey—the most important one in the archdiocese. It was utterly demolished by the troops of Louis XIV in the seventeenth century, but recent excavations beneath the reconstructed monastery have unearthed evidence of the great church built in the time of Saint Martin, in the fourth century, on the spot where Maximinus had been buried.

It is moving to think that eight hundred years later Hildegard of Bingen, the nun and mystic who left a legacy of so many works that are being rediscovered today, on being invited to preach in the cathedral of Trier, must have visited the Basilica of Saint Maximinus and the tomb of the saint. Indeed, she composed a sequence about him that has come down to us—one of the more beautiful of her musical compositions, the one beginning with the words *Columba aspexit*: "The dove perceived through the spaces in the lattice the fragrant balm of Maximinus, the resplendent one. . . ."

It is possible, if not probable, that Martin was acquainted with the bishop, Saint Maximinus of Trier. That would explain the events that would follow in the course of his life, for we find him again in Poitiers, in the very center of Gaul; now Saint Maximinus was originally from Poitiers, his brother Maxentius was bishop of that town, and it was while going to visit him there that Maximinus died, in 347 or 349 (the date cannot be determined precisely).

In any event, we find Martin in Poitiers, to which he was drawn by the reputation of the bishop who succeeded Maximinus and whose name was Hilary. This travel back and forth between two such distant cities might seem surprising, but let us not forget that both cities at the time were spiritual capitals and, more concretely, transportation centers, destinations of the roads carved out by the Roman legions.

The man whom we call Saint Hilary of Poitiers was born in that town around the year 300 (the exact date is unknown). He had received a substantial education, notably at Bordeaux, which was at that time, as we have noted, an intellectual center of the first order. He himself related, in the first book of his treatise entitled *De Trinitate*, how he had been converted by reading the beginning of the Gospel according to Saint John: dissatisfied with pagan doctrines about human destiny, he had literally been dazzled by "the Word, the true light which enlightens every man", and who gave to all men "the power to become children of God". He dedicated himself impetuously, then, to studying the Word of God and received the sacrament of baptism. Although he was married and had a daughter named Abra, he was admitted to priestly orders, and it was not long before he was appointed a bishop. It happened rather often—this was the case with Paulinus of Nola, as we have seen—that holy orders were conferred in this way upon married men, who then followed the counsel of Saint Paul: "Let those who have wives live as though they had none" (1 Cor 7:29). Thus we find bishops who with regard to their wives, as Saint Jerome described them, "cease to be husbands". It was not until the end of the fourth century that Pope Siricius (384–399) would [explicitly] require celibacy of all clerics. Again, this decision would be confirmed several times before the Lateran Council in 1123, which would [officially] impose the discipline upon the entire Western Church.[1]

Hilary was renowned far and wide, both as a man of God and as a churchman, when he was called to succeed Maxentius in the episcopal see of Poitiers. This reputation, no doubt, was what drew Martin to Poitiers at the moment when the prospect of a new life was opening up for him. Having just spent so many years in the military, which is by no means conducive to solitude and recollection, he sensed that he needed a guide in his vocation to the ascetical, solitary life.

Hilary received him with joy, and even proposed to make him a deacon immediately, but Martin refused; he did not feel that he was worthy of the honor or the responsibility. Hilary only managed to convince him to become an exorcist, which was a very lowly office, equivalent to that of a porter, among the minor orders that eventually lead a candidate up to the priesthood.

Was this the first step in the new life that he had hoped for so much? He thought so; but once more destiny would arrange things otherwise. On the eve of embarking upon a life consecrated to silence and prayer, Martin considered it his duty to go and find his parents so as to bid them farewell. No doubt he had received news of them from time to time as the years went by; he knew that both of them had returned to his native Pannonia, to the village of Sabaria. Sulpicius Severus assures us that he decided on the basis of a dream to make this journey—and there is nothing improbable about that. Whether a dream or a deliberation, it seemed to him a logical step, since he was preparing to bid farewell to the world.

---

[1] The development of the celibacy requirement is treated here in terms of decrees rather than traditional practice. See Stefan Heid, *Celibacy in the Early Church* (San Francisco: Ignatius Press, 2000).—TRANS.

When he made his plan known to Hilary, the latter warmly encouraged him, while making him promise to return.

A journey like that could not be made without some difficulties. They started when Martin attempted to cross the Alps, perhaps at the pass called Little Saint Bernard, or to travel through the Cottian Alps by the saddle of Mont Cenis. "First, he lost his way in the Alps and fell among brigands. One of them lifted his axe and poised it for a blow at his head, but the other one checked his hand as he was striking." He was bound and led off, since one of the robbers wanted to interrogate him to find out whether he had encountered any wagon along the way, a merchant, for example, whom they could plunder. Martin himself could hardly be of interest to them: he no longer wore the splendid uniform of the imperial guard, but a worn tunic instead, and he did not carry much baggage at all. The robber began by asking him who he was, to which Martin replied that he was a Christian. "Aren't you afraid?" "But he declared with the greatest firmness that he had never felt safer, since he knew that the Lord's compassion is never closer than when the trial comes."

In other words, the robber struck up a conversation with the man who was traveling alone on foot, and it took a turn that certainly surprised the former. In this passage of the biography, Sulpicius is most likely reporting incidents as Martin himself remembered and related them. Martin began to lament the lot of the brigand, telling him that the plying of his unhappy trade rendered him unworthy of the mercy of Christ; whereupon the thief to whom he was speaking must have asked for explanations, which Martin was eager to give him. Finally, the robber set Martin loose, asking him to pray to the Lord for him. Sulpicius Severus assures his readers that subsequently this brigand converted and began to lead an exemplary life, and that he himself had told the story of his meeting with Martin.

Upon arriving on the plains of Italy, not far from Milan, Martin had another encounter, one that left an indelible mark on his life. A man he met on the road asked him, "Where are you going?"

Martin answered, "Wherever the God is calling me."

"Then wherever you go," said he, "and whatever you attempt, you will have the devil against you."

To which Martin answered in the words of the Prophet: "The Lord is my helper; I shall not be afraid of what men may do to me" (Ps 117[118]:6). Immediately the man who had barred his way disappeared.

Martin knew that he had been dealing with the devil. Many people today no longer believe in the existence of the devil, but in his day there was no difficulty in admitting what the Bible teaches: that malicious powers exist that seek to separate the creature from his God. *Dia-bolon* is a Greek word meaning "one who separates", and it is interesting to contrast this term with its opposite, *sym-bolon*, the symbol, something that brings together. Is there a negative being that leads a life that is likewise negative, that tends to separate man from his Creator? This remains a question posed by an age of faith. Nowadays we know that there is a disease, cancer, which manifests itself as a negative form of life, a life that counteracts life. This could be a striking metaphor for what happens in the spiritual life.

Other occasions would present themselves for Martin to contend with the interior enemy he called the devil. For the moment, he continued his journey over hill and over dale, until he reached the city of Sabaria, which he could scarcely recognize, where he was welcomed, however, in the house of his parents. Any son might want to see his father and his mother again, but above and beyond the hope of seeing them again was the desire to bring them to the faith that had been his for a long time now. But his father would have nothing to do with that.

And he had good reasons, we must admit. "People who flatter themselves on finding the true faith should start by agreeing on what it is! Maybe then we'll be able to believe them! What a spectacle they make of themselves now: people tear each other apart, think only of taking sides, endlessly debate the questions that divide them, and sow discord and dissension everywhere."

These objections were overwhelming but true, as Martin was all too painfully aware. The fourth century had seen the Church emerge from the underground; now people hoped that the Roman Empire would become Christian, an easy inference to make, since they were accustomed to seeing the emperor, who exercised supreme authority throughout his domain, make decisions about the spiritual life of his subjects. That could only open magnificent prospects for the Church: the religion of the emperor, the religion of the empire. Didn't this herald the new age that was in the offing? The age of Christ's glorious return, for which the Roman legions would, so to speak, pave the way?

Now, in the middle of the fourth century, quite unexpectedly, the Church was being torn apart instead. Of course there had always been heresies; Saint Paul himself had already warned against those who were proclaiming a gospel different from his. But the role of the Churches and of the successor of Peter consisted precisely of bringing back to the straight and narrow path those who were in error. They were to preach untiringly the true faith in God the Father, the Son, and the Holy Spirit. And now this fundamental belief was under attack. Ever since around the year 323, a priest from Alexandria by the name of Arius had been in open rebellion against his bishop, Alexander. His main concern was to preserve somehow in the theology that he set forth the fundamental character of God the Father, who, as he vehemently claimed, was the sole truly eternal, truly unbegotten being, the only true principle of all beings. The Word, the Logos (that is, the Christ), had received life and being from Him, Arius said, and had been created as a perfect, divine creature, before all ages, but only the Father, in his view, was true God.

This teaching had been debated not only in the city of Alexandria, but throughout the Church in Egypt. Alexander hastened to convene a council consisting of around a hundred bishops, all of them from Egypt or Libya, which anathematized the error of Arius and excommunicated him, as well as his adherents. There was only a small group of them anyway: five priests, six deacons, and two bishops.

But Arius did not accept that condemnation. He appealed to various bishops, notably in Palestine; among others, to a profoundly learned individual, Eusebius of Caesarea; and also to another Eusebius, from Nicomedia, who was very influential with the emperor. Those bishops convened synods that gathered in Palestine and in the province of Bithynia, rejected the decisions made by the Council of Alexandria and the anathemas that had been hurled at Arius, and rehabilitated the latter. It was an exasperating situation, as you may well imagine, in all ecclesiastical circles; even more seriously, the conflict extended beyond them. The bishops who were hurling anathemas at one another displeased the emperor; hence the decision to convoke a general council, what we call today an ecumenical council.

It was the first one in history. At Constantine's orders, and with his support—to facilitate travel he granted them the right to use imperial post-horses—three hundred bishops gathered in Nicaea on May 20, 325. This council was to compose a "symbol", a sort of summary of the faith, in which the three Persons of the Holy Trinity were clearly and precisely enumerated: the Son being "God from God, Light from Light, True God from True God, begotten, not made, consubstantial [one in being] with the Father". Thus the contents of the faith were neatly defined. Of all the bishops present, only two rejected this new definition.

The emperor was satisfied, but after the council the debates just got louder instead of subsiding. Complications followed that would often be repeated over the course of history: the interference of the temporal power in purely religious questions would aggravate matters and finally affect the life of the Church.

For Emperor Constantine, only three years after Nicaea, adopted a new point of view—probably due to the influence of his half-sister, Constantia, who was very much attached to the doctrines of Arius. The latter was called back from exile and rehabilitated, and his teachings continued to spread. One of his adversaries, Athanasius, who had become the bishop of Alexandria and had passionately defended the definition of the Council of Nicaea, was soon exiled by the same Constantine. After the emperor's death in 337, his successors took turns siding with one cause or the other. This happened at a time when the structure of the Roman Empire itself was beginning to weaken, and armies did not stop short of proclaiming whomever they wanted as emperor, so that the doctrinal confusion was aggravated by political confusion.

The partisans and adversaries of Arius kept hurling their anathemas at each other. So it was that Saint Athanasius spent the greater part of his life outside of his diocese; exiled five times, now to Trier, then to Rome, sometimes to Egypt, he died in 373 without having seen the end of a crisis that would leave lasting marks, especially in the East, and that spread from gatherings of theologians to the entire Christian population. Gregory of Nyssa, for instance, relates, "Whenever you went to the money-changer, to the butcher's shop or to the thermal baths, people asked you whether the Father is greater than the Son, or whether the Son proceeded from nothing!" In other words, the theological dispute deeply divided the Christian world.

It even extended to several peoples who knew the gospel only from the preaching of Arian heretics. Indeed, in the year 341 a man named Ulfila was raised to the episcopacy; his family had been seized and carried off by the Goths during their first invasion as far as the shores of the Black Sea. Ulfila, though Christian, was an Arian; he understood perfectly the Gothic language and customs; he carried on intense missionary work among the Germanic peoples, going so far as to develop a new alphabet in order to transcribe Sacred Scripture for them. Furthermore, most of the invaders who settled in Europe—the Visigoths, the Ostrogoths, and the Vandals—were acquainted with the Christian religion only in its heretical Arian form. Ulfila followed the trend that had prevailed in the East and had been ratified in 359 by the Council of Rimini, where the Arian profession of faith had triumphed. Thus the Germanic world, like many regions in the East, was drawn into a heresy that would persist for a very long time: about three centuries.

As for western Europe, when Clovis, King of the Franks, rejected paganism in 496 at the prompting of his wife, Clotilde, and chose the Catholic religion, France was proclaimed the "eldest daughter of the Church". Other nations, Spain, for example, were slow to repudiate the heresy to which the Visigoths had converted. Moreover, the Arian crisis had left deep scars on the Churches in the East, where other heresies began to multiply.

And so Martin found his father's objections somewhat disarming. His mother gave him a more favorable hearing; he had the joy of bringing her to the Christian faith. It wasn't long, moreover, until he himself experienced the trouble that heresy can cause: the violence with which its partisans were confronting adherents to orthodoxy. In that region along the Danube, which in those days was called Illyricum—the eastern extreme of the Roman Empire—the bishops, on the whole, had adopted Arianism—three of them in particular, Valens of Mursa, Germinius of Sirmium, and Ursacius of Singidunum, in three cities located between one hundred and one hundred fifty kilometers [between sixty-five and one hundred miles] from Sabaria. Martin, who had opposed one of those bishops and his clergy, was beaten with rods and had to flee.

Emperor Constantius himself supported the heresy. At that time he had left Italy and had traveled via Rimini and Ravenna toward the vicinity of Trent and the Danube region. In the month of October in the year 356 he was at Sirmium, and he did not leave that region until two years later, in order to go to Constantinople, then to the East, where he died, in 361. In that same city of Sirmium he had induced a council of Arians to draw up a sort of charter of their heretical teachings, which he managed to have signed by the bishop of Córdoba, Ossius, who had formerly championed the Council of Nicaea. It is true that Ossius was quite elderly by then and that members of his entourage accused him of having become "delirious" on the subject. In other words, the entire region—under the influence of the emperor, please note—was becoming Arian. It is not surprising, therefore, that Martin was driven out of it.

Now, upon arriving in Italy, he learned that Hilary, for his part, had had to leave Poitiers and was also in exile, and that Rhodianus, the bishop of Toulouse, and Liberius, the bishop of Rome, had likewise been exiled, due to the influence of a fierce proponent of Arianism, Saturninus, the bishop of Arles.

Martin stopped in Milan, which was hardly the thing to do in his situation: indeed, the bishop of that city, Auxentius, another Arian, and his clergy, who had been won over to the heresy, wasted no time in banishing the traveler.

What was he to do? Where could he go? No doubt the time had come to carry out the plan he had always dreamed of and live an ascetical life in seclusion. Across from the coastal city of Albenga there was a little island called Gallinara, which seemed to offer a satisfactory retreat. Another priest, whom Sulpicius does not name, accompanied him in his exile. The two of them went off, then, like the monks in Egypt, to live on wild herbs and prayer. There can be no question about the priority of prayer in Martin's life, but in the wild herbs department he was somewhat lacking in experience: he very nearly poisoned himself with one sort that Sulpicius mentions. The plant was hellebore, which, administered in small doses, was then considered a remedy for madness, but which is quite poisonous when ingested heedlessly. The biographer says that Martin "met the threatening danger with prayer and at once all the pain vanished".

Once he had recovered from his poisoning, he learned that Hilary had been authorized to go back to his episcopal see. Indeed, as Sulpicius Severus explains, Hilary had received orders to return to Gaul, even though the sentence of exile had not been revoked. Evidently the authorities preferred to keep him under surveillance in his own diocese rather than let him continue engaging in theological jousts in other local churches, which did not always have happy results for his adversaries. Martin went first to Rome, where he hoped to meet Hilary as the latter made his way back to France; but since the bishop had already left, Martin had to travel the road to Poitiers again. Finally he would be able to begin the ascetical life he had always wanted to lead, but that one could not embark upon without some preparation—as his experience on the island of Gallinara had proved: to live on wild herbs you have to know what they are!

Furthermore, Martin had good reason to meditate on the terrible rift that divided the Church. No sooner had she been liberated, called to live in the daylight under the protection of the "temporal powers", than a terrible new situation had come about. Errors and heresies had been around since the age of the apostles; now, however, the divisions were becoming more pronounced and violent precisely because of the interest that the temporal powers were taking in the Christian faith. The Gospels say it plainly: "Do not think that I have come to bring peace on earth; I have not come to bring peace, but a sword. For I have come to set a man against his father, and a daughter against her mother, and a daughter-in-law against her mother-in-law; and a man's foes will be those of his own household" (Mt 10:34–36; Lk 12:51–53). This harsh prediction was coming true, then, and the emperors, by intervening in the life of the Church, unceasingly aggravated the situation—especially during this period when the empire was beginning to break up. The appeals of the bishops of Rome (starting with Saint Clement) to strive for unity, "so as to watch over the health of this body that we form in Christ Jesus", were becoming urgent. When faced with the Arian heresy, more than ever before, it was important to watch over the health of this body.

Martin knew instinctively that such evils could be remedied only by prayer. In order to pray better, in order to learn how to dedicate his time and his energies more effectively to listening to God, he would henceforth have a guide in the person of Hilary.

Almost immediately after his arrival in Poitiers, his dream of a hermit's life became a reality. The biographer says that Martin settled not far from the city in a hermitage, traces of which have been preserved to this day. It is located less than ten kilometers [about six miles] from Poitiers, on the banks of the Clain, in Ligugé. There Martin was not far from his master and friend, Bishop Hilary, and yet could devote himself to prayer in what was then a deserted place.

Martin, however, did not remain alone for long. Soon other Christians, drawn as he was to a life of prayer, gathered in Ligugé, an indication of what would be built there later on, a Benedictine abbey, which still stands in our day. (The monks who were driven from it in 1901 returned in 1919. Let it be noted in passing that their abbey is distinguished for its magnificent library.) In a rapid development, therefore, the man who had settled down to be a hermit started to lead the life of a cenobite—that is, a life in community. Of course his lodgings could not house them all, and numerous "cabins" were constructed by disciples who were anxious to imitate him. These were probably the sort of buildings made out of cut stones that one finds in all Celtic lands, from Ireland to Provence in the south of France—where, as late as the eighteenth century, shepherds used to build *bories* without any mortar and, by cleverly heaping stones one upon the other, managed to construct little houses that were perfectly waterproof.

In modern times excavations have been carried out in Ligugé. As a result, in 1954 archeologists discovered underneath the present-day church a seventh-century crypt and, a little farther on, the remains of a Gallo-Roman residence that had been built at the place where Saint Martin worked his miracles, which is called the *Martyrium*.

It is very likely that Hilary had succeeded in convincing Martin to receive major orders, and that consequently he had become a deacon, then a priest. One day a catechumen came looking for him, wishing to be instructed in the faith and to receive baptism. This man abruptly fell sick and had violent bouts of fever. "Martin happened to be away at the time." He would occasionally leave Ligugé in this way, probably at Hilary's request, but these absences were of short duration. He returned after three days and found his catechumen lifeless, surrounded by Martin's companions, who were grieving and preparing to bury the man. We will let Sulpicius Severus tell the story:

> With his whole soul possessed by the Holy Spirit, [Martin] ordered the others out of the cell where the body lay, fastened the door, and stretched himself out over the lifeless limbs of the dead brother. For some time he gave his whole self to prayer. Then, made aware by the Spirit of God that divine power was present, he raised himself a little, fixed his eyes on the dead man, and awaited without misgiving the outcome of his prayer and of the Lord's mercy. Hardly two hours had gone by before he saw the dead man stir slightly in all his limbs, then blink, as his eyes opened again to see. Then indeed he turned to the Lord with shouts of gratitude and filled the cell with the sound of them.

Martin's companions could not help being drawn by the noise, and they gathered on the other side of the door. "And what a marvellous sight! The man they had left dead, they saw alive."

The *Martyrium* in Ligugé is said to have been built later on the site of this resuscitation, which recalls the example of the prophet Elisha in the Old Testament (2 Kings 4:33ff.), when the prophet revived the son of the Shunammite woman. The catechumen who had been brought back from death to life was baptized soon afterward and remained

among the disciples of Martin in Ligugé. Sulpicius Severus
gives us to understand that the man testified gladly to his
resurrection in answer to Martin's prayers. He writes:

> He lived for many years afterwards. He was the first among us
> to be the subject of Martin's miracle-working and to bear
> witness to it. He was in the habit of relating how, when he
> was out of the body, he had been brought before the tribunal
> of the Judge and had heard the dismal sentence of consign-
> ment to a place of gloom among the generality of men. Then
> two angels had represented to the Judge that he was the man
> for whom Martin was praying. He was therefore ordered to
> be taken back by these same angels and to be restored to
> Martin and to his former life.

A similar miracle took place on another occasion. Martin
was traveling through the domain of a certain Lupicinus,
when he heard cries and lamenting. He approached the village to find out where they were coming from, and an inhabitant explained that a slave boy had just committed suicide; he
had hanged himself. "Hearing this, [Sulpicius relates,] Martin
went into the hut where the body lay, shut everybody out,
laid himself upon the body and prayed for a while. Presently
the dead man's features showed signs of life and his faded eyes
looked into Martin's face." The man sat up, took the hand of
the stranger who had just saved him, and managed to stand.
Then, "with all the crowd looking on, he walked with him
up to the front of the house."

Two resurrections. Perhaps in our day one would speak of
"resuscitations". They are striking nonetheless. Probably Martin was the least astonished of them all at what had taken
place: he had prayed, and God had answered his prayer. He
had always known how attentive God is to the prayers of his
people. His reputation spread no less rapidly as a result.

Sulpicius Severus, moreover, relates the facts without mentioning the word "miracle", which the bystanders most certainly would have used in this regard.

He does not elaborate on the events that may have taken place within that setting of Ligugé, under the aegis of Saint Hilary of Poitiers, but it is not that difficult to conjecture what the conversations between such a master and such a disciple would have been like. Martin wrote nothing, but we have two precious works by Saint Hilary, the commentary on the Gospel of Saint Matthew, *In Mattheum*, and, more important, the treatise on the Trinity, *De Trinitate*. "I pray Thee, Lord, keep my fervent faith undefiled", he exclaims in the latter work—and that must have been Martin's prayer as well, in an age when the faith was being attacked at its origins, since the Arians went so far as to deny the divinity of Christ. No affirmation was forceful enough, in Hilary's estimation, to do justice to the One God in Three Divine Persons:

> For my part, [he says,] so long as I shall have the power by means of this Spirit Whom Thou hast granted me, Holy Father, Almighty God, I will confess Thee to be not only eternally God, but also eternally Father. Nor will I ever . . . assert that Thou wast ever without Thy Wisdom, and Thy Power, and Thy Word, without God Only-begotten, my Lord Jesus Christ. . . . He is the Son, a Son born of Thee, God the Father, Himself true God, begotten by Thee in the unity of Thy unbegotten nature. . . .
>
> I must also deny that this name of "creature" belongs to Thy Holy Spirit, seeing that He proceeds from Thee and is sent through Thy Son, so great is my reverence for Thy mysteries. . . . I possess the reality that I believe, though I comprehend it not.

And Hilary marvels once more that he was "born again" when he was baptized, in the name of the Father, and of the Son, and of the Holy Spirit.

Such testimonies, born of the controversies that abounded in that age, allow us to observe, so to speak, the development of doctrine, which progresses not by way of successive additions, but through gradual elaboration. Ultimately, the heresies would bring about progress in the expression of the faith during those early centuries known as the "patristic period" (named after the Fathers of the Church). More deliberate in his actions and achievements than Athanasius, Hilary made a magnificent contribution to his age, of which Martin was a beneficiary. During the years that he spent in Poitiers, no doubt, conversations about Christian doctrine took place, which made it a productive period in Martin's life, as well as in the life of the Church. Thus we find that even the heresies that sowed division and fomented discord among the various Christian communities had in the final analysis a positive side to them, in that they forced the Church to define her doctrines precisely.

This would prove true throughout the life of the Church, but especially in the fourth century, which for her was the start of a process of maturation. While the Arian crisis was developing, another was taking shape that would one day have an importance that was unsuspected at the beginning. The ideas in question were those of Apollinaris of Laodicea. This fervent proponent of the Nicene Creed—which set him apart from many Christians in the very heart of Syria, which was to a large extent Arian—professed that Christ, the God-man, nevertheless could not have been a man entirely like other men, and he denied his two natures, divine and human. Apollinaris had been condemned during a synod in Rome presided over by Pope Damasus in 377. Yet his error provoked endless discussions, which were prolonged in the condemnations later pronounced against Nestorius, the bishop of Constantinople. The latter was incensed, in particular, about the title "Mother of God" given to the Blessed Virgin by the piety of the faithful—a title that is documented in Egypt as far back as the late third century.

The century following Martin's was full of impassioned investigations into the Person of God the Son. Saint Cyril of Alexandria put forth great efforts to demonstrate the twofold nature of Christ in the unity of his Person. The Council of Ephesus in 431 and the one in Chalcedon twenty years later (451) resounded with the controversies that arose on this subject; not all the Churches accepted the decisions of these councils, particularly in the East, where various schismatic tendencies developed, which Emperor Justinian later attempted to subdue, although some of them persist to the present day. One example is the so-called "Jacobite" or Syrian Monophysite Church, with which an ecumenical dialogue was nevertheless begun in the twentieth century.

Martin later had the opportunity, as we will see, to take part in some of these debates that arose over the more or less proven departures from the faith of one thinker or another. His own position was first and foremost that of a believer who receives the deposit of the faith rather than seeking to discuss the elements of it. For him, the faith is light, and contemplation leads to the fullness of knowledge.

We must emphasize, furthermore, how productive his century was, again from the perspective of the faith: besides the heated discussions and the divisions that they brought about, many local Churches sprang up, testifying to an ardent evangelization, such as the Armenian Church—influenced by Saint Gregory the Illuminator—which converted King Tiridates at the end of the third century. It was during the fourth century that this Church, once it acquired an original alphabet for its language, translated Sacred Scripture and received the Christian liturgy. She continued to adhere to it despite persecutions, especially by the Persians, over the next centuries.

A little farther to the north, in Georgia, a woman called Saint Nino (perhaps a diminutive form of Christiana) converted the royal family, King Mirian and his people. In Ethiopia the Christian faith was introduced in the fourth century by two young men, Frumentius and Aedesius. Originally from Tyre in Phoenicia, they were shipwrecked and cast upon the shores of Abyssinia, where they set about preaching the gospel. In the capital city of Aksum, Frumentius became the first bishop of a Church that was destined to emerge unscathed by the heresies of the age.

3

The Bishop of Tours and the Church of His Time

The death of Hilary of Poitiers was experienced throughout Christianity as an immense loss. The great theologian disappeared at the moment when Arianism was only gaining ground. For Martin it was a heavy blow: at the same time that he lost a friend, a pioneer along this way of asceticism on which he had set out, he was losing his most reliable counselor—one who, at a time when heresy was disturbing the Church so drastically, was able to proclaim the truth clearly and to defend the faith.

That was when they came to sound Martin out and propose that he become bishop: the third bishop of the city of Tours, whose people had just witnessed the death of Lidoire, the successor of Gatien, who had inaugurated the episcopal office in that city. That tells you how young the Church of Tours still was. Furthermore, there were only twenty-two bishops in all of Gaul around the year 317, at the time when Martin was born; there were seventy at the end of the century, which implies a vigorous development of the Christian life.

Martin, who had once refused to become a deacon and for a long time had put off accepting the burden of the priestly ministry, was not going to let himself be convinced that easily to become a bishop; he felt that he was completely unworthy of such an office.

After saying that he refused, he received a visit from an inhabitant of Tours named Rusticius. The man fell to his knees and begged him to come visit his sick wife. Martin agreed and set out on the journey: to travel from Poitiers to Tours took about three days on foot. After a while, the road became rather congested: a crowd had joined Rusticius, and their numbers increased, the closer they came to the city. People from Tours had gathered there, and even some from the nearby cities. Martin, literally a captive of the throng that surrounded him, realized that he had walked into an ambush. "All [of the bystanders] had the same desire and the same opinion, which was that Martin was the fittest to be bishop and that the Church would be fortunate to get such a priest."

Once again he would be obliged to do something he had not wanted to do: he would be a bishop in spite of himself. And this would take place in circumstances that bordered on the comical, for his biographer notes that not everyone was in complete agreement about this nomination: in particular, some of the bishops who had been called on for the occasion. This helps us to imagine the sort of conspiracy that had been formed—the countless meetings and, no doubt, the impassioned discussions—in order to get him to come to Tours. The banks of the Loire River must have seen a great many rendezvous and heard numerous arguments both for and against. Although the agreement seems to have been unanimously expressed by the voice of the people, some objections had been raised nevertheless by a few of the bishops: "They said, if you please, that Martin was a despicable individual and quite unfit to be a bishop, what with his insignificant appearance, his sordid garments and his disgraceful hair." We can imagine what Martin looked like, since contemporaries repeatedly emphasized his unkempt appearance, the worn tunic; he probably had no use for a hairdresser.

But perhaps this is precisely the thing that won for him the devotion of the people. Martin was, even in his appearance, the opposite of those worldly prelates of whom Saint Jerome has left us a merciless portrait: "Such men think of nothing but their dress; they use perfumes freely, and see that there are no creases in their leather shoes. Their curling hair shows traces of the tongs; their fingers glisten with rings; they walk on tiptoe across a damp road, not to splash their feet." We must imagine Martin in a coarse woolen tunic, his hair in disarray—but that is probably why the people instinctively appreciated him.

We might also, at this juncture, ask how the crowd was dressed. For clothing, too, evolves. Certain people in that century, especially in the upper classes, wore the Roman toga, which was long and cumbersome. Some men, mainly among the common folk, wore a shirt, with Gaulish breeches or trousers, while the women wore skirts; both sexes wore a cape (another custom handed down by the Celts), which covered the head and shoulders, offering protection from the sun, the rain, and the cold, and which would become very popular in the centuries to come.

Thus we can imagine the throng gathered in the cathedral. . . . The other bishops were there, obliged to proceed to the consecration ceremony that would make Martin one of them. And then there was a comic episode. The one who protested the most against this nomination, wrested from them by main force, was the bishop of Angers, a certain *Defensor* or "Defender".[1] The biographer says that he was

---

[1] *Defensor* in Latin can mean either "defender" or "one who wards off, averts". Sulpicius Severus did not give the name of the bishop in question.— TRANS.

"the chief opponent". The ceremony was about to begin, but it turned out that the lector who was supposed to start off with some liturgical readings had not managed to make his way through the multitude. We can imagine the expectant crowd, the tense, tumultuous atmosphere. "In the confusion among the ministers during the wait for the absentee, one of the bystanders picked up a psalter and plunged into the first verse he saw. It was: 'Out of the mouths of babes and sucklings thou hast brought praise to perfection, to destroy the enemy and defender.' When these words were read, the congregation raised a shout and the opposition was put to shame."

The Book of Psalms, opened at random, caused this humiliation of the aforementioned Defender, who was stubbornly opposed to Martin, and silenced him! We might reflect for a moment on this action, mentioned in many anecdotes, of a person who is in doubt or in distress opening the Bible and considering what he reads by chance on the open page to be God's answer. In this case the passage was Psalm 8, verse 3, a well-known psalm, since the Gospel records that Christ himself made use of it to tell the Pharisees, in the presence of the children who were acclaiming him, "Out of the mouth of infants and of sucklings, thou hast perfected praise because of thy enemies" (Douay-Rheims). "It was generally thought that God had prompted the reading of this particular psalm in order that Defender should hear its condemnation of his proceedings. For while the praise of the Lord had been brought to perfection out of the mouths of babes and sucklings in the person of Martin, he himself [*Defensor*] had been exposed as an enemy and destroyed at the same time."

That is how, in spite of himself and in spite of certain members of the episcopacy, Martin became the bishop of Tours.

The account of this turbulent election—which can very probably be dated Sunday, July 4, 370—plunges us into the very heart of the Church of that time, in which, as we see, the *vox populi* played an important role.

In a certain sense, it was during this fourth century that the life, the liturgy, and the structures of the Church were taking shape. During the first three centuries, even though she had begun to take root to some extent everywhere in the Roman world, both in the West and in the East, the Church led a great part of her life underground: the catacombs testify to this, and the dominant feature of that ecclesial life remained the cult of the martyrs, the splendid "witnesses" to a faith that was proclaimed against the civil authorities, despite torments, and even in the jaws of savage beasts. With the fourth century and the official recognition of the Christian faith—or, rather, its adoption by the emperors, beginning with Constantine—another era commenced, raising the hopes of all those who had embraced the Christian faith. Now, in broad daylight, they watched buildings go up in which this faith was affirmed. The emperor himself had churches built, for instance, the Rotunda in Jerusalem, which would mark for all ages to come the location of Christ's tomb and thus the place of the Resurrection.

Yet at the same time they saw everywhere the outbreak of those divisions that we have mentioned. And since the emperor, acting as ruler in the religious domain, as in everything else that depended on the imperial power, lent his support to some of the factions, the consequences were considerably more weighty. Thus, in the Churches of Africa, the schism of the bishop Donatus caused deep rifts among Christians. Now, as things developed, the schismatic groups were sometimes opposed by Constantine, sometimes tolerated or even encouraged by him and his successors. And everywhere the

Arian crisis—it, too, winning in turn the opposition and the encouragement of the temporal authority—resulted in deep divisions, which would become worse and worse over the centuries, given that the successive waves of invaders, as we have seen, for the most part had embraced Christianity in its heretical form. It was disconcerting, nonetheless, for those in the following [i.e., the fifth] century who saw the break-up of the empire, on which so many hopes had been set.

Already, at the close of the fourth century, the emperor's situation was not the same as it had been at the time of Diocletian. That sovereign—the last, merciless persecutor—had set up two empires, one in the East and the other in the West, each one headed by an emperor and a "caesar". This was to cause a great deal of trouble in imperial history, especially since the armies, which were becoming the most effective force in an age when the civil authorities were losing their prestige, had no scruples, it has been said, about naming emperors to suit their soldiers. History is full of such incidents even in Martin's day.

His day was also the time in which Christian life became firmly established and was deepened. That era saw the birth of a Christian culture: meditation on the Bible and continual prayer sustained by the psalms occasioned a cultural development that would be fully manifest in future centuries, whereas the liturgy that was being elaborated then would give birth as well to musical forms, even to surprising theatrical forms. All of that was only germinating during the century in which Martin lived. But while the pagan culture, which for some time had been seeking to renew itself by means of various esoteric influences, was becoming impoverished, a Christian culture was beginning to unfold and starting to flourish even in that period. That century has been called the golden age of the Fathers of the Church. Indeed, thinkers, writers, and preachers enriched Christian literature as never before with brilliant achievements.

Furthermore, it was during that same century that the Church in the East recognized some of her greatest apostles—starting with Saint Basil, the "wonder of the world", as some of his contemporaries called him. Originally from Cappadocia, having been born around 329 to a very wealthy family, he studied at Constantinople, then in Athens. Early in life he was attracted to the ascetic life, but an asceticism untainted by Manicheanism (which was inspired by a disdain for the body); in this he distinguished himself from many of his rivals in the East and resembled Martin, who practiced corporal penances in moderation for the sake of the contemplative life. Like Martin, Basil, who was ordained a priest in 364, had disciples who had gathered around him. During the severe famine in the year 368, he founded hospices for the sick and the needy. In 370 he became bishop of Caesarea in Cappadocia. Throughout his lifetime, in the voluminous correspondence he carried on with the many people who sought his advice, he constantly drew from Scripture and Tradition fresh insights with which to confront the assaults of heresies, in particular that of the Arians. He died in 379.

A quite different career was that of his younger brother, Gregory of Nyssa, who was born around 335. More intellectual, more anxious and combative as well, he would be considered "the most universal theologian of his century". With his *Great Catechism* he left to the Church "the first great attempt at a doctrinal synthesis of the Christian faith".[2] Although he was married, he nevertheless dedicated his first scholarly work to a treatise entitled *On Virginity*. He became bishop of Nyssa in 371 and experienced several setbacks, was

[2] Hans von Campenhausen, *Les Pères grecs* [The Greek Fathers] (Marbach, 1983), p. 184.

removed from office and exiled, then reinstated in 378. He participated in the Council of Constantinople in 381, in spite of attacks from the opponents of the Nicene Creed, and on two occasions he was invited to deliver the funeral orations for exalted personages of the imperial family. He wrote a biography of Macrina, his sister, and also the life of Basil— both men owed much to the highly enlightened piety of their older sister, who had gathered into a community virgins dedicated to the contemplative life. Gregory of Nyssa died in 394.

Gregory Nazianzen, born around 330, was a friend of the two brothers, but especially of Saint Basil, from whom he was inseparable; the two studied together. Gregory, who was endowed with a refined literary taste, was fond of Homer and Virgil. Son of a priest, he became a priest himself, then bishop of Sasima in 372, but he carried ineptly the burden of an office for which he was scarcely suited. Eventually, called from seclusion by those who had remained faithful to the decisions of the Council of Nicaea against Arianism, he served as bishop of Constantinople for a time, having been appointed by Emperor Theodosius (Christmas, 380). Various conflicts arose, forcing him to retire to Nazianzus, where he died in 389 or 390, leaving numerous poetical works.

Those are the principal "Greek Fathers", the glory of the fourth century. To them should be added John Chrysostom, whose life encroaches somewhat upon the following century: born between 344 and 354, he died in 407.

In the West, it was the age of Saint Jerome, the patron of scholars. Then finally comes the best-known of all, Saint Augustine, the influence of whose thinking has never been disputed. All of these great names, eminent personalities whose works form the lasting basis for theology or, more broadly speaking, for Christian doctrine, flourished during the second half of the fourth century or in the first half of the following century. We should add another bishop, who did not seek the episcopal office any more than Martin did, but whose subsequent influence was as strong as his personality: Saint Ambrose, bishop of Milan, with whom the Church learned to sing. He enriched that local Church with an extraordinary legacy, composing hymns and sequences of great beauty that contributed to the formation of Gregorian chant.

Like Saint Martin, Saint Ambrose had been brought to the episcopacy by popular acclaim, although in noticeably different circumstances—just as their "social situations", we might say, were different. His father was prefect of the Gauls; he himself, although he had little interest in official duties, and even less in rhetoric, had been placed in charge of the province of Æmilia-Liguria [in modern-day northern Italy] and became its governor at the age of twenty-nine. In order to carry out his duties and restore order in the city of Milan, he went to the cathedral church of that city in 374, upon the death of the bishop, Auxentius. Two candidates disputed the claim to succeed the departed ordinary. Ambrose was busy trying to pacify their electors, when suddenly a child in the crowd called out, "Ambrose for bishop!" Everyone repeated the cry, so that reluctantly and despite his protestations he had to acquiesce (though not without first attempting to flee). He was not yet baptized; within one week he received baptism and all the minor and major orders, finally becoming a bishop at the age of thirty-four. Later on he was to baptize Saint Augustine, who was consecrated bishop of Hippo in 395. Ambrose once had the occasion of leading the emperor Theodosius to repentance and of requiring him to make reparation after the murders that he had ordered at Thessalonica. But above all his influence was profound and lasting as concerns the liturgy.

For this is what distinguishes the Christian from all others: the liturgy, participation in eucharistic worship. For the most part it is a daily service, which is celebrated more solemnly, however, on Sunday, or even on both Saturday and Sunday, as in Egypt. The Church was also beginning to organize the liturgical year in its entirety, with the obvious high point being the Solemnity of Easter. In preparation for it, the Church observed a forty-day period, recalling the forty days during which Christ fasted at the beginning of his public life—a period that is then extended by feast days corresponding to the Jewish feasts of that same season, leading up to Pentecost. There were differences between the Churches of the East and of the West as to the dates of these feasts, because the method of reckoning was not the same everywhere. In the Western Church, moreover, other distinctive customs would be established, notably in the fifth and sixth centuries, when the Churches in England and in Ireland began to assume a place of importance. A decision of a council would be necessary to assure that Easter would be celebrated on the same date as in the Roman Church; this would be accomplished in 664 to 665, at the Council of Whitby, under the aegis of Saint Hilda.

The winter feast days in the East were also slightly different from those celebrated in the West. The Eastern Churches developed the custom of celebrating the appearance or manifestation of God on earth on January 6: this was the feast of the Epiphany or the "Theophany", which would soon be adopted in all the local Churches. At Rome, in the fourth century, shortly before the year 336, they began to celebrate the Nativity on the twenty-fifth of December. Emperor Aurelian had attempted in 274 to institute a pagan feast in honor of the unconquered sun, *Sol invictus*. With the triumph of the Christian Church, this *Sol invictus* became the figure of

Christ, the true Sun of justice, and little by little the feast of the Nativity, which was destined to become so popular, spread to all the local Churches.

The councils did not delay in imposing upon Christians the obligation to participate in the Eucharistic Sacrifice, which gathers the people in church before the altar. Communion under both species (of bread and wine) was the rule for those who attended Mass in those days. But from the fourth century on, Christians seemed to be less diligent about attending. In the year 400 the Council of Toledo threatened with excommunication those Christians who allowed three or four Sundays to go by without coming to church.

Although the liturgical celebrations sometimes varied a bit from one local Church to the next, the Eucharistic Sacrifice remained the essential component. One important modification, however, was introduced, again in the fourth century, which was so productive. Indeed, until then the language of the Church had been Greek, the *Koiné* used at the time of Christ, which was the common language of the people in various parts of the empire, and which for a long time would remain the language of culture and scholarship. From the end of the third century, however, Latin—a popular form of the language used by soldiers who came from different regions and had a more or less mixed heritage—was in use, and little by little it prevailed throughout the empire. This form of Latin was adopted by the Church—to the great indignation of some of her members, for instance, the priest Hippolytus, who was so outraged that Latin was being substituted for Greek that he vehemently attacked the bishop of Rome and had himself excommunicated. Ultimately he was reconciled with Pope Callistus; sent off to the mines of Sardinia, he ended his life there and died a martyr. Around that same period, Tertullian resolutely made use of Latin in his writings. Soon nothing remained of the early Greek liturgy except the invocation *Kyrie eleison*, which has lasted to this day [and the *Hagios o Theos*, which is still an option in the Good Friday liturgy]. In the same way, the liturgical prayers have retained several Hebrew terms: Amen, Hosanna, Alleluia.

But it was not until the beginning of the fifth century that, thanks to the labors of Saint Jerome, the entire Bible was translated into Latin and could from then on be used by all of the local Churches in the West. Pope Damasus, who did much to foster the use of Latin in the liturgy, enthusiastically encouraged Jerome, his former secretary and collaborator, to undertake this work. Damasus had been elected in the midst of serious difficulties in 366, and he was an influential force in the fight against the Arians. At the same time he had an ongoing interest in the life of the Church during the age of the persecutions and commissioned what we would call archeological investigations in order to discover the tombs of the martyrs; this research continued until his death in 384. We have seen already in the West that Saint Ambrose had the congregation in Milan sing in Latin and that he introduced the use of Latin hymns.

Latin remains to the present day the official language of the Church, but the difficulties that arose after the Second Vatican Council when vernacular languages—English, French, German, as well as Korean, Bantu, and Tamil, etc.—were introduced make it easier to understand the difficulties that might have arisen during the early centuries of the Church, when Latin was just being introduced as a liturgical language.

In all other respects, during the fourth century the main features of liturgical life were already established. The essential act of worship remained the Eucharist, the consecration of bread and wine, normally performed by the bishop in the presence of the priests, who were gathered around him.

There was no longer any talk of *agapés*, the fellowship meals that took place during the apostolic age, for even then they were marred by the disorders against which Saint Paul protested.

Conferring baptism was still, more often than not, the duty of the bishop. On the days before the ceremony, in general on Friday and Saturday, the candidates for baptism would fast. At the end of that fast, there was a solemn rite of exorcism; then the bishop breathed on the face of the candidate and made the Sign of the Cross on his forehead, ears, and nose. Then baptism was administered: a triple immersion, which underscored a triple profession of faith. When there were children among the candidates, they were baptized first. Women had to approach the sacrament with their hair down [i.e., loosened, not braided]. The bishop then placed his hand upon the baptized person, poured consecrated oil on his head, and traced the Sign of the Cross on his forehead. The baptized person then received the kiss of peace; from then on he was allowed to pray in church with all the other Christian faithful. The bishop consecrated the bread and wine that the deacons presented to him; he also blessed a mixture of milk and honey that would be offered to the newly baptized, along with a cup of water. It was not long before the sacrament of confirmation was distinguished from that of baptism and constituted a separate rite. Each one of these rituals intro-duced the Christian into the community in a concrete way.

The other sacraments, too, received names. Thus in the letters of Saint Ignatius of Antioch, written in the early years of the second century, we read: "It becomes both men and women who marry, to form their union with the approval of the bishop." Tertullian, in the third century, extolled Christian marriage: "How can we adequately describe the happiness of that marriage which the Church bonds, and the oblation confirms, and the blessing signs and seals; to which angels testify, and which the Father ratifies?"

The reconciliation of sinners is also the object of a discipline; it is recognized as a true sacrament. According to the seriousness of his faults, the penitent may be excluded for a rather long period of time from the fellowship of believers. The rituals and conditions for his reconciliation, moreover, gave rise to impassioned discussions during the third century.

At any rate, an abiding and essential part of Christian life is the practice of the three things prescribed by the gospel: fasting, almsgiving, and prayer.

As for death, it is accompanied by prayers and blessings and is followed by a burial ceremony that attests to the hope of a future life. From the fourth century on, tombstones proclaim in this way the Christian faith in a supernatural destiny. This is revealed by Christian inscriptions in Gaul, which have been methodically researched and restored by the CNRS (Centre National de la Researche Scientifique) under the aegis of Henri Marrou and published beginning in 1975. A series of excavations was conducted at Trier, the results of which were published by Nancy Gauthier. This great city on the Moselle River, which during the reign of Constantine became the second capital of the empire after Rome, has yielded an important number of burial plaques, most of them Christian, some of which go back to the fourth century, in the two necropolises that were excavated, one to the north and the other to the south of the city. The inhabitants used to bury their dead *extra muros*, outside the city walls. Many Christians hoped to be laid to rest *ad sanctos*, near the tombs of the saints who had gone before them in this life; researchers have also discovered a number of sarcophagi and tombstones near the tombs of Saint Paulinus and of Saint Maximinus, north of the city.

Most of the inscriptions (more than half) include symbolic characters following the texts that say who is buried under the *stela* and mention the relative, the father, mother, spouse, children, who made the arrangements. For example: "To my dearly beloved wife Aurora, faithful Aquilinius"; or in another inscription: "To Memorius, her very dear husband, who lived thirty-seven years, Festa has posted [this epitaph]; in peace"; or again: "Here lies Amanda, an innocent child, who lived one year, six months, and nine days." None of these inscriptions is dated, but most of them are accompanied by a chi-rho monogram—the Greek letters X and P, the first two letters of the (transliterated) Greek word KRISTOS (Χριστ ϕ)—interwoven with crosses or doves, often portrayed beside a tree or pecking at a vase. Thus we find two doves and an olive tree at the bottom of the inscription that says: "Here rests in peace Martina, a very sweet young girl [*dulcissima puella*] who lived sixteen years and a day; her parents posted this epitaph." Quite often one also finds the cross or the chi-rho, or both, inscribed within a circle; or the circle with a cross on either side, or flanked by doves, sometimes by branches bearing grapes. Specialists date the epitaphs in question to the fourth century—the time of Saint Martin—or to the beginning of the fifth century. The chi-rho becomes less common from the fifth century on, then it disappears.

Some of these inscriptions, among the most ancient ones, include the term *neophita*, neophyte, which means a newly baptized person. From this it has been inferred that some of these Christians had themselves baptized on the point of death. We know that this was the case with Emperor Constantine, who in 337 died clothed in his neophyte's robe.

The morals of the common people changed noticeably, in comparison with the brutality of the preceding centuries. An edict of the Senate prohibited all infanticide in 374. In the society of that time Christians had always attracted notice because, as the letter to Diognetus explains, "They keep all of their children." In another area, the same fourth century witnessed the first protests against the cruel games, such as the fights between gladiators of which the pagan mob was so fond.

But the story of Martin draws our attention especially to the procedure by which he was made a bishop; indeed, it is quite surprising for us twentieth-century [twenty-first-century] Christians to see the participation of the people on that occasion. Surprising on two counts: on the one hand, because today the bishops of the hierarchy alone decide, with the approval of the pope, on the nomination of new bishops; on the other hand, because of the interest the people took in that particular nomination. These two reasons allow us to take a closer look at the age in which Martin lived, that century when civil society was slowly but surely becoming a Christian society.

Saint Cyprian specifies "that the one who is to govern a diocese should be chosen by the neighboring bishops in the presence of the people, and that he should be deemed worthy by public acclamation". The canons of the Council of Nicaea require the presence of at least three bishops, and in fact we see the local bishops giving their opinion with regard to the nomination of Martin—even when the opinion in question is negative, like that of the *Defensor*, the bishop of Angers.

It is remarkable on this occasion that the Christian populace could tell perfectly well what the real qualifications of a bishop are and what character traits indicate that a person possesses those qualities. The inhabitants of Tours cared very little about the fact that Martin was not well-coiffed; on the contrary, they were very much aware of his reputation for piety and of his love of poverty. At that historical moment one might have foreseen the proverb that would be current many centuries later, during the medieval period: "Golden crozier, wooden bishop; wooden crozier, golden bishop."

The story allows us to infer the existence of a close-knit Christian community gathered around its bishop and making considerable demands on him. Already in the latter half of the second century, Irenaeus, bishop of Lyons, had trenchantly defined the role of the bishop as opposed to that of the founders of sects, which at that time were numerous. Members of sects impose their doctrines upon themselves and upon others, whereas bishops act to preserve the common faith.

> Now all these [heretics] are of much later date than the bishops to whom the apostles committed the Churches. . . . [T]hese heretics, since they are blind to the truth, and deviate from the right way, will walk in various roads; and therefore the footsteps of their doctrine are scattered here and there without agreement or connection. But the path of those belonging to the Church circumscribes the whole world, as possessing the sure tradition from the apostles, and gives unto us to see that the faith of all is one and the same, since all . . . preserve the same form of ecclesiastical constitution.

That is precisely the common trait that Christians saw then in their bishops, and this is in keeping with the demand for unity that they expected of them. The bishop was the guardian of the faith, whatever his personal qualities and skills might be in other respects, and the bishop of Rome, the successor of Peter, was already considered the one who was supposed to intervene when the faith was at stake. His ministry is ordered, above all, to the welfare of the entire Church. In a period when heresies were sowing discord, beginning with the doctrines of Arius, it was important for the bishop to stand up for right doctrine, the teaching of the apostles. The enthusiasm shown by the populace came from their recognition that Martin was genuinely holy and, at the same time, a righteous disciple of Hilary. Furthermore, the bishops of the region ratified their choice.

This popular movement also heralded an age during which the episcopal office would take on additional importance. In fact, at the turn of the fourth century, cracks began to appear in the imposing apparatus of the imperial administration. We have seen that Diocletian had supposed that he could preserve the vast empire by divvying up the authority: two emperors, two caesars. This already presaged the division that would set in between the western empire and the eastern empire. Constantine united them again under his rule, but a reestablishment of this sort could not last long: at his death in 337, there were no longer two but three sons who divided the empire among themselves. From then on, every so often an emperor would declare himself the sole ruler over the empire: Constantius in 351, Julian the Apostate ten years later. Again, Theodosius, who at first was emperor of the East (378), declared himself the sole emperor, but that was shortly before his death (395). A few years later, the barbarians captured Rome: in that year, 410, the campaigns of Alaric brought about the collapse of the empire—a process that was completed in 476 when the last "Roman emperor" was deposed, who by a historical irony was named Romulus Augustulus. The barbarians definitively conquered the Roman world, and it would take no less than the immense talent and profound insight of Saint Augustine to make the Christian world accept the crumbling of the hopes it had pinned on a temporal Christian empire.

In practice, as a result of these successive upheavals, that solid Roman system of governance which was supposed to be indestructible was shaken; from then on it was like a ship taking on water on every side, and finally it disappeared. To whom could the people turn? Who would protect the multitudes who were literally left to fend for themselves? As it happened, the hierarchy of the Church remained the sole source of stability; the ascendancy of the temporal powers, which was such a threat to her in the fourth century—at the time of the Arian crisis, when the emperors were exiling the heretical bishops one minute and the faithful bishops the next—was now a thing of the past. For a time one might have believed that all of Europe was going to become Arian, for the Goths, the Visigoths, and the Vandals had been won over to Arianism. That was when Clovis, the chief of the Franks, the only invading people that was still pagan, chose to be baptized into the Catholic faith. Hence the great importance of that baptism (which probably took place in the year 496, or perhaps in 499, at Christmastime); hence, too, the nickname that the bishops who had remained true to the trinitarian faith would give to France: "the eldest daughter of the Church".

With the hindsight of history, we can project all of this back, like a superimposed image, on the consecration of Saint Martin. It occurred precisely during that pivotal era, and it helps us to understand the dependence of the people upon their bishop, which subsequently would characterize the episcopacy of [Saint] Sidonius Apollinaris [bishop of Clermont] and also, much later, a bishop of Paris like Gozlin, who was battling against the Normans. . . .

In other words, the bishop was becoming an important personage in the city. Not exactly an official, but someone to whom you could turn, a voice that could make itself heard and would speak up in defense of the powerless. This development coincided with the moment at which the city became Christian. From the year 325 on, Sunday was an official holiday, whereas the pagan feasts were no longer celebrated officially. The only one among them that persisted was the first of January. The birthdays of the emperors were also celebrated in the territory ruled by each one.

At the same time, the gladiator fights became less frequent and, little by little, ceased altogether; they were forbidden in theory as early as 325, but in fact continued for almost a century. Battles between men were replaced with fights against wild animals; later on there were exhibitions in which skill prevailed over violence, just like in the modern-day circus. It was not until the nineteenth century that brutality would reappear, in the form of boxing matches.

Very early on, the bishops made efforts to redeem slaves. Besides the mass emancipations carried out by [Saint] Melania, the wife of Bishop Pinian, and by [Saint] Paulinus of Nola, we should recall the easy terms offered by bishops for freeing slaves: a simple statement made in the presence of the bishop was enough to free a slave, and this act was officially valid. Likewise there was a concerted effort to mitigate the treatment of prisoners. Thus in the Theodosian Code, as scholars have noted,[3] seven laws were passed between 320 and 409: the first forbade jailers to allow prisoners to die of hunger; the last one obliged them to bring their charges to the public baths "once a week, on Sunday".

Subsequently there were several efforts to ameliorate the lot of the most unfortunate. First and foremost we must mention the project of Fabiola, about which Saint Jerome speaks: she is credited with the invention of the hospital, a house where the sick are cared for, a *nosokomion*, one of those fortunate inventions destined to endure for centuries

[3] J. Daniélou and H. Marrou, *Nouvelle histoire de l'Église* [A new history of the Church] (Éditions du Seuil, 1927), vol. 1, p. 383.

and that still has its place in our world today, as anyone can tell you. At the same time, the senator Pammachius, who also was a convert, founded near Ostia a hospice for pilgrims, a *xenodochium*, welcoming those who might disembark weary or sick at the port of Rome, to which they were traveling on pilgrimage. The Eastern Church had already seen Saint Basil establish a "poor house" around 372 in Caesarea in Cappadocia.

All of these institutions springing up, little by little, are inseparable today from the very idea of a civilized state. It does not hurt to recall from time to time that they owe their existence to the Church, which from the earliest years of her liberation multiplied her attempts to combat sickness, infirmity, and other ills that burden humanity.

Another feature of civilization originated and developed in this century, which was so promising and produced so many initiatives: pilgrimage. We should note that, unlike what happened a few centuries later in Islam, pilgrimage does not constitute a ritual act in the Christian religion; it does not even merit a place in the liturgy. Nevertheless, it exerts a powerful attraction, and in the fourth century no one suspected how important it would be in the development of the culture and the civilization that we call "medieval". The day would come when people in great crowds would embark on long journeys, thus creating unexpected exchanges, causing hospitals and, in even greater numbers, churches to spring up at stopping places, and changing the roads along the great trade routes. For example, in western France, there would eventually be a road that one could call the *Chemin de Saint-Jacques*, the "way of Saint James", used by those who were on their way to the shrine at Compostela in Spain.

Now it was during the fourth century that the custom of going on pilgrimage arose and developed. It had been prescribed by the Jewish religion to go to Jerusalem in order to celebrate the Passover there, but medieval pilgrimage is of a completely different character. People would go to visit a holy place: Rome, Jerusalem, and, from around the seventh or eighth century on, what was supposed to be the tomb of the apostle Saint James in Compostela. But as early as the fourth century, they traveled to the holy places around Calvary or to Old Testament sites to honor the memory of Abraham at Hebron or of Moses at Mount Sinai, or sometimes to pay a visit to individuals whom they admired, such as the hermit Saint Anthony of the desert or Saint Pachomius, who created "monastic" community by gathering disciples who wished to share his life of asceticism.

Concerning one of these early fourth-century pilgrimages, from Bordeaux to Jerusalem, we possess a written itinerary dated 333; there is also the very famous pilgrimage that has gone by the titles of *Peregrinatio Silviae* and *Peregrinatio Etheriae*.[4] It is the true account of a pilgrimage made by a woman, a nun, no doubt, who went to Jerusalem probably toward the end of the fourth century (the date 395 has been suggested), and who seems to have made her departure from Aquitaine as well. Modern textual criticism has given its own version of her name, "Egeria", to this woman who composed a genuine travelogue, the most ancient record of this sort. Thoroughly imbued with a passion for Sacred Scripture, she climbed Mount Horeb to see the site of the burning bush; she drank at a spring that was thought to be the one Moses caused to stream from the rock, and thus she multiplies her references to both the Old and the New Testaments. This account, by itself, would be enough to demonstrate (if there were any need to do so) that women were at least as numer-

---

[4] See E. Franceschini and R. Weber, *Itinerarium Egeriae*, in *Corpus christianorum, Series latina*, vol. 175 (Brépols, 1965).

ous as men in hastening along the pilgrimage routes—and that this was true from earliest antiquity.

Let us recall, furthermore, that it was to a woman, the mother of the emperor Constantine, Saint Helena, that we owe the investigations that resulted in the discovery of the True Cross of Christ—the most important relic that drew pilgrims to Jerusalem. She was seventy-eight years old when she traveled, in 325, to the Holy City. It is well-known that during the Roman occupation a temple to Venus had been erected upon the site of Christ's sepulchre. A manuscript dating back to the eighth century, which is preserved in the cathedral of Vercelli in Italy, explains how the empress, in the course of the excavations she commissioned on the site of Calvary, discovered three crosses, with the help of a converted Jew who happened to be named Judas.[5] The discovery is celebrated on September 14, the Exaltation of the Holy Cross (in some languages it is called the feast of the "Invention" of the Cross, from the Latin word *invenire*, which means "to find"). A basilica was constructed on the site, and it was consecrated on September 14, 335—therefore during the lifetime of Saint Martin. This basilica was the ultimate goal of the pilgrimages to Jerusalem in his day.

---

[5] Michael Hesemann, in his voluminous book *Die Jesus-Tafel* (on the inscription over the Cross of Christ), painstakingly sorts out the legendary details (e.g. the convert "Judas") from the historical facts of the discovery of the True Cross by Saint Helena.—TRANS.

4

The Bishop in His Diocese

Once Martin becomes the bishop of Tours, the biography of
Sulpicius Severus has an abundant supply of anecdotes. Martin, who in no way sought a position of authority, who did
not even accept the episcopal ministry until after a veritable
ambush, nonetheless did not fail to put it into practice as soon
as he took office. And it is impressive to see the zeal with
which he immediately strove to guide the piety of the faithful
entrusted to his care, by speaking up against all the errors that
might cause them to stray.

To begin with the historical errors: it is significant that we
see him grappling first with a tradition that was considered
venerable, but that was nevertheless false:

> Not far from the town . . . there was a place to which sanctity
> had been mistakenly attributed with the idea that martyrs
> were buried there. There was even an altar there, erected by
> previous bishops. But Martin did not lightly give credence to
> uncertainties, and made constant efforts to get from the older
> priests and clerics the name of the martyr and the occasion
> when he suffered. . . . No certain and settled tradition had
> come down to them.

Consider that this was an era when the desire to honor the
memory of the martyrs sometimes prevailed over a concern
about precise information.

Far from joining in the devotion that the faithful of his diocese were lavishing on the aforesaid tomb, Martin remained suspicious. For him, the cult of the martyrs demanded more than simple hearsay. We can only commend his concern for the truth, which over the centuries has been lacking in so many people, whether religious or not, with regard to relics and stories of various kinds. We will let his biographer narrate the incident:

> For some time, therefore, he kept away from the place, not condemning the cultus, since he was not sure of his ground, but at the same time not lending his authority to popular opinion, in case he should be strengthening a superstition. Then one day he took with him a few of the brethren and went to the place. Standing on the grave itself, he prayed to Our Lord to make it known who was buried there and what his character had been.

That was when, according to the chronicle, he saw "a ghost standing close by, foul and grim". The person in question was a robber who had been executed for his crimes, who was mistakenly venerated by the common folk but had absolutely nothing in common with the martyrs. Those who accompanied Martin heard the voice but saw nothing. "Martin now described [publicly] what he had seen and gave orders for the altar which had stood there to be removed. Thus he rid the population of a false and superstitious belief."

It is impressive to find this incident related at the very beginning of his episcopate: it is in fact the first act that is reported after his installation in Tours. And it is of interest to us as well to note Martin's pursuit of truth at the start of his ministry. Clearly, Martin had a sense of history and a respect for it: After all, of what interest is history unless it is the search for what is true? Too often piety has been confused with superstition, and not only in Martin's day! This is the appropriate moment to acknowledge his sense of history, which is indispensable in distinguishing truth from falsehood.

We should note that similar vigilance was required, in his era especially, from the religious point of view: the common folk were still pagan, at least in their customs and their everyday reactions, and Martin would take great pains to help them distinguish truth from error, in particular with respect to religious matters, by battling against the idols and demystifying idolatry.

Sulpicius Severus recounts in several places how Martin repeatedly dispelled superstitions. The people were still pagan, and the temples that the Romans or the Gallo-Romans had built were still there. Every time he had the opportunity, Martin destroyed these temples and the statues that adorned them. Not without running into trouble sometimes. What happened in Levroux (in Indre, some distance from Châtillon) is quite characteristic in this regard. There was a pagan temple there "which had been made very rich by its superstitious cult". Martin challenged the inhabitants of Levroux to demolish it, but, as Sulpicius Severus relates, "he met with resistance from a crowd of pagans and was driven off with some injuries to himself." Martin did not insist. He had recourse instead to his usual plan of action: prayer. He withdrew to a secluded place and for three days,

> [clothed] in sackcloth and ashes, continuously fasting and praying, he besought Our Lord that the temple which human hands had failed to demolish might be destroyed by divine power. Then suddenly [his biographer writes] two angels stood before him, looking like heavenly warriors, with spears and shields. They said that the Lord had sent them to rout the rustic host and give Martin protection, so that no one should hinder the destruction of the temple.

Martin returned, therefore, to the village and started again his assault on the statues and altars of what Sulpicius Severus calls "the heathen sanctuary". And the crowds watched him without budging. No one threatened him. They just let him carry out his work of demolition. "The sight convinced the rustics that it was by divine decree that they had been stupefied and overcome with dread, so as to offer no resistance to the bishop. . . ." And by reasoning that might appear simplistic but that nonetheless is consistent with the psychology of crowds, they concluded that Martin's God was the one they should adore, not the idols, who in this instance had proved incapable of defending themselves.

The story would repeat itself, to be sure, in various circumstances; in fact, the unusual thing about Martin was that he did not wait until the peasants in his diocese came looking for him but, rather, went out to meet them. And, as his biographer explains, "he immediately built a church or a monastery in every place where he destroyed a pagan shrine." These pagan shrines had become numerous especially during the centuries of Roman rule. The Gauls had quite easily adopted several of the gods from the Roman religion—Mercury, for example—and the public worship or "cultus" practiced by the Romans, an essential element of colonization, had led to great numbers of temples and statues. For Martin, as for Christians in general, it was important to obliterate the memories of an idolatrous cult that he condemned. But in many cases, as at Levroux, the populace could not understand this zeal against the shrines where they had long been accustomed to gather for official ceremonies.

Some of the prodigies that accompanied the work of Martin in these instances are still famous today. Once he set fire to "a very ancient and much frequented shrine in a certain village". This is the sort of language used in a biography that does not always furnish the precise information that we would expect nowadays. In any case, the fire threatened to spread to nearby houses. The chronicle continues: "When Martin noticed this, he climbed speedily to the roof of the house and placed himself in front of the oncoming flames. Then you might have seen an amazing sight—the flames bending back against the force of the wind till it looked like a battle between warring elements." Martin's word, his stance, subdued the elements: "The fire destroyed only where it was bidden." Evidently this was a sight that left a lasting impression on the eyewitnesses.

On other occasions, Martin had to undergo more direct attacks, as in the incident that took place one day "in the country of the Ædui".[1] As the chronicle of Sulpicius Severus notes (with its usual annoying lack of precision), the moment Martin began to demolish the temple, "a frenzied mob of rustic pagans made a rush at him and one of them, more audacious than the rest, drew his sword and went for him. Throwing back his cloak, Martin offered his bare neck to the stroke. Nor was the pagan slow to strike but, when his hand was well above his head, he fell flat on his back. Stricken with the fear of God, he asked for pardon."

The episode in Amboise, which seems to have taken place as he was beginning his apostolate, is no less striking. "In the *vicus Ambatiensis*" (Amboise), Sulpicius writes (*Dialogues* 3, 8), specifying: "In the old fortress, now the home of a large community of monks, there used to be the shrine of an idol. It was a vast and solidly-built edifice—a towering mass of highly polished stones, tapering into a lofty cone; and the grandeur of the work did much to keep superstition alive in the locality." It was surely a Roman temple. The narrator continues:

---

[1] "Eduen country" refers to the district around "Augustodunum", present-day Autun, which is quite distant from Tours.

The man of blessings had frequently given Marcellus, the priest resident in the place, orders for its destruction. Returning there after a considerable interval, he took the priest to task because the idolatrous building was still standing.

The priest's defence was that the pulling down of such a massive structure would be difficult enough even with the employment of troops or with the aid of a state labour-force; certainly one could hardly imagine that it could be carried out by some feeble clergy and sickly monks.

So Martin resorted to his familiar aids and spent all night in prayer. In the morning a storm arose that razed the idol's temple to its foundations.

Sulpicius hastens to add, "Marcellus can witness to what I have been telling you."

In order to convince the reader, he adds another account of the same sort. He relates the incident, he says, according to the testimony of his friend Refrigerius:

Martin was proposing to throw down an immensely massive column on the top of which an idol stood, but there were no means available for carrying out the plan. Then, in his usual way, he resorted to prayer. It is a certain fact that another column something like the first came hurtling down from heaven and hit the idol and crushed to powder the whole invincible mass. It would seem that it was too small a thing that Martin should employ the powers of heaven invisibly; the powers themselves had to be seen by human eyes visibly doing Martin's will.

These stories acquaint us with one aspect of evangelization in the fourth century: it was a question of demonstrating the power of God, even in the physical realm, by doing away with the idols in which the common folk had trusted until then.

Thus Martin, when he acted as a demolition expert, was protected by divine power. One day someone tried to stab him with a knife while he was intent on destroying idols, but, the chronicle tells us, "in the very act of striking, the weapon was struck from his hand and disappeared."

All of these anecdotes showing Martin protected by an interior force, while contending with a crowd that was still pagan, reveal to us what was characteristic of his activity as a bishop. In fourth-century Gaul evangelization was carried out essentially in the towns; in that era they were the centers of activity to which government and civilization gravitated. Once a certain number of Christians lived in a town, a bishop was appointed who, with his entourage of priests and deacons, was responsible for religious life in that locality. We have seen that at Tours the bishop had not been appointed until a rather late date, since there had only been two of them, Gatien and Lidoire, before Martin.

And what did Martin do? He traveled all around the countryside; that is where he met the pagans; that is where the shrines dedicated to the idols still existed. Although a liturgical life was being led in the towns, the rural areas were left almost entirely to themselves; judging from the signs of hostility that he encountered, Martin must have been going well beyond the customary confines of a bishop's ministry. His evangelization efforts even led him far from his diocese, if you consider Levroux or that district which belonged to the "Æduen country" but is otherwise unnamed (the Ædui were the peoples who inhabited the lands between the Saône and the Loire Rivers, with the plateau of Autun at the center). Thus, from the earliest records of his episcopate, he was traveling well beyond the boundaries of his "diocese". And that would be characteristic of his ministry: he unceasingly went about the *pagi*, the remote rural areas inhabited by peasants, far from the main roads, which were also the principal avenues of evangelization.

And so we see him, not only boldly attacking these shrines—unpretentious temples decorated with those statues of which the Romans were so fond—but also going to the very heart of the Celtic religion, which still had such a powerful hold on the souls of the Gauls. It is better understood today that the Celts, rather than adoring Jupiter, Juno, or Minerva, had a religion oriented to the forces of nature. Scholars tell us that they venerated springs and trees, in other words, manifestations of life, such as gushing water or the sap that flows in the trees. In Martin's eyes, this reverence for life was insufficient; obviously, he tried to bring the people from animism to an awareness of a transcendent life. The incident of the pine tree illustrates this endeavor.

One day, in a village that the author once again unfortunately does not name ("in a certain village"), Martin was attacking a pagan monument that he describes as "very ancient": a pine tree, which significantly was located quite near a shrine where people still worshipped, since the narrative speaks of "the priest of the place". In fact, it might have been a shrine to Cybele, the mother-goddess, whose cult persisted for a long time in the empire, which was gradually being Christianized: it has been remarked that several altars dating from the end of the fourth century and dedicated to the mother-goddess have been discovered in the course of excavations at the Vatican. That is to say that this cult harmonized with the cult of the sacred trees, which were so dear to the Celts. Now we read that the peasants of that locality watched calmly as their temple was being destroyed, but suddenly grew angry when Martin attacked the pine tree. The chronicle puts it quite clearly: "These same people had been quiet enough, at Our Lord's command, while the temple was being thrown down, but they were not prepared to see the tree felled." We can discern in this attachment to the sacred tree what was at the bottom of the religion of the Gauls.

But Martin intended to continue his work and strike at the animism that was so deeply rooted among the peasants who surrounded him. One of them then challenged him: "If you have confidence in the God you say you worship, stand where the tree will fall, and we will cut it down ourselves; and if your Lord, as you call Him, is with you, you will not be harmed." Martin accepted these unusual terms, and from that point on the chronicle depicts for us in minute detail the events that unfolded before the eyes of the crowd of pagan peasants, on the one hand, and of Martin's companions, on the other hand—monks who must have gone with him on his missionary expeditions. The narrative continues:

> And as the pine leant to one side, so that there was no doubt on which side it would fall when cut through, Martin was bound and made to stand on the spot chosen by the rustics, where they were all quite sure that the tree would come down. Then they began to cut down the tree themselves with great joy and delight. A wondering crowd stood at a little distance.
>
> Gradually the pine began nodding and a disastrous fall seemed imminent. Standing at a distance, the monks grew pale; and, so frightened were they as the danger drew near, that they lost all hope and courage, and could only await the death of Martin. He, however, waited undaunted, relying on the Lord. The tottering pine had already given a crack, it was actually falling, it was just coming down on him, when he lifted his hand and met it with the sign of salvation.
>
> At that—and you would have thought it had been whipped like a top, the tree plunged in another direction, almost crushing some rustics who had ensconced themselves in a safe place.

The miracle occurred in public and was plain to see. Moreover, it would be long remembered, and from then on, with regard to Martin, people would speak about the felled pine almost as much as about the cloak. The effect that it had on the bystanders was gripping:

> Then indeed a shout went up to heaven as the pagans gasped at the miracle, the monks wept for joy, and all with one accord acclaimed the name of Christ; and you may be sure that on that day salvation came to that region. Indeed, there was hardly anyone in that vast multitude of pagans who did not ask for the imposition of hands, abandoning his heathenish errors and making profession of faith in the Lord Jesus.
>
> It is certainly a fact that before Martin's time very few, in fact hardly anyone, in those parts acknowledged the Name of Christ.

It was absolutely a miracle, and also testified to Martin's mission in all sorts of regions, which the reader can follow in the later passages of the chronicle; he devoted himself untiringly to preaching to the little people, to seeking out in their own settlements those who did not come into town.

One could sum up Martin's apostolate by noting that he did not take the Roman road but, rather, the Gaulish byway. And in doing so he converted multitudes, rescued them from animism, which to some extent is the peasant's natural religion; this was no doubt the most important part of his ministry. Martin displayed inexhaustible fervor. Quite literally, he was on the road constantly, and it is significant that the French word for "way" or "route", *chemin*, comes from a Celtic term—like several other rural vocabulary words in French: *rucher* (beehive), *arpent* (acre), *charrue* (plow), etc., which retained their Gaulish forms, as did the vocabulary of French geography in its totality, since all the names of rivers and most city names are derived from Celtic words.

Among these encounters with the peasantry, we must cite another that is almost comical, because an error Martin made became the basis for a miracle! The story is worth transcribing exactly as the chronicle relates it:

> Some time after this he happened, when on a journey, to encounter the corpse of a pagan being carried to its grave with superstitious rites. He had seen the approaching crowd from a distance and stopped for a little, not knowing what it was, for there was nearly half a mile between them and it was difficult to distinguish what he saw. He made out, however, a band of rustics, and linen cloths (that had been spread over the body) fluttering in the wind. He supposed, therefore, that unhallowed sacrificial rites were being performed, for it was the custom of the Gallic rustics, in their lamentable infatuation, [Sulpicius Severus tells us,] to carry round their fields the images of the demons covered with white veils. With uplifted hand, therefore, he made the Sign of the Cross before the approaching crowd and ordered them not to move from where they were and to put down what they were carrying.
>
> Then indeed there was a wonderful sight to be seen. First the unfortunate creatures turned as rigid as rocks. Then they tried with all their might to advance but, being quite unable to move forward, they kept turning round in the most ridiculous whirligigs. Finally, completely beaten, they put down the body they were carrying and, looking at one another in their bewilderment, silently speculated as to what had happened to them. However, when the man of blessings found that the assemblage was a funeral procession and not for sacrifices, he raised his hand again and set them free to pick up the body and go on. Thus, when he wished, he made them halt and when he chose he let them go.

The anecdote is amusing in itself, and it shows that even when he was mistaken, Martin was capable of having an effect on a crowd. And his biographer concludes by adding that, even in those instances when the peasants showed some hostility when they saw him destroying their shrines, "he so subdued their pagan hearts by his holy preaching that the light of the truth penetrated to them and they themselves threw down their own temples."

Actually, this was the only negative part of his ministry. The temple symbolized error; the thing was to convince the inhabitants not only to renounce the false gods and the accompanying mythology that had been introduced by Roman rule, but also to transcend the deeper animistic beliefs that had characterized the religious thinking of the Celts, and to bring them to recognize a source of life other than the one that makes the trees grow and the springs gush. In return, chapels would often be set up subsequently near trees and springs, since the transition from the life of nature to a sense of a divine life was no longer a problem for the converted people. The passage from a natural life to a spiritual life took place precisely in Martin's time.

We repeat that this was the negative part of Martin's life: attacking idols. Every era has its idol; in Martin's day they were to be found in their most visible form; they were still named Jupiter, Mercury, or Venus. Later on, they would assume other forms, in which they would no doubt be more difficult to discern as idols: power, money, sex. And Martin's battles prefigured those the Church would have to wage in other instances—according to the circumstances, with more or less skill, relevance, or determination to have done with them—against the multifarious idols that are constantly springing up again. The story of Martin presents this battle to us in what we might call the most obvious form. At any rate, he vigorously went on the attack.

During this campaign against the idols, Martin inevitably met the one who inspires them. And it is worth reading those pages relating how Martin confronted the devil or those whom he had possessed—the anecdotes from his life that may appear the most difficult to accept in our day. The best thing to do, it seems, is to take note of them just as they are presented to us, even though we may arrive at conclusions different from the ones drawn by his biographer.

So it is with the episode of the slave belonging to Tetradius. The latter was "a man of proconsular rank", the chronicle tells us, that is, a highly placed personage who played an important role in the city. One of his slaves was possessed by a demon, and Tetradius asked the bishop to impose his hands upon him. Martin ordered the slave to be brought to him, but the possessed man was undergoing such a violent crisis that he hurled himself like a madman at those who were trying to make him leave his cell. Consequently Tetradius begged Martin to come himself into the house where that cell was located. The bishop hesitated; could he, being the bishop, go "to the unhallowed house of a pagan"? Tetradius, who was obviously attached to his slave, "therefore promised that, if the demon were expelled from the boy, he would become a Christian", so Martin granted his request. He went into his house, placed his hands upon the young slave and drove the demon out. Let Sulpicius Severus tell the end of the story in his own words: "Tetradius, on seeing this, made profession of faith in the Lord Jesus. He became a catechumen at once and was baptized not long afterwards. He always cherished an extraordinary affection for Martin as the instrument of his salvation."

Soon afterward Martin worked another cure of the same sort, but this time for the head of a household with whom he was acquainted. The moment he set foot in the man's house, he declared that he saw a frightful demon in the courtyard. Now this demon manifested itself in the person of the householder's cook. "The unhappy man began to gnash his teeth and to maul everyone who approached him." Whether it was a fit of madness or a case of possession, everybody fled, terrified by the furious creature. Martin alone took up a position in front of him. "But he still kept gnashing his teeth and opening his mouth to bite." Martin then thrust his fingers into the man's mouth, saying: "If you have any power at all, devour these." And the possessed man, instead of clamping his teeth down on those fingers, kept his mouth open, "as if he had a red-hot iron between them". The account adds that, since the demon inside of that man could not go out through the mouth, it was discharged by breaking wind. This scene describes a case of possession where some might see a bout of madness caused by internal maladies. The fact remains that the enraged man was cured.

Another case of demonic possession: a rumor had spread to the effect that the barbarians were at the gates, about to invade the city. Now Martin—this happened, the narrator remarks, "before everybody in the cathedral"—commanded a possessed man who was present, and whom he had recognized as such, to say plainly whether this news was true. The man declared that ten demons had helped him to spread a false rumor among the populace, hoping by that subterfuge to make Martin leave his city. Thus the bishop "freed the city from the disquieting fears that had been overhanging it".

5

Along Highways and Byways

It is impressive to see that Martin, upon becoming bishop of Tours, in no way abandoned what had been his primary concern from the earliest days of his life: prayer and contemplation. While he was living not far from Hilary in Poitiers, some catechumens and some baptized Christians had gathered around him, attracted by him as well as by a life of prayer, and a sort of community was formed at Ligugé, on the banks of the River Clain.

Once he was settled in Tours, he inspired still other contemplatives, individuals who were drawn by prayer and flocked to him, so that they constituted the beginnings of a monastery. Indeed, he himself sought to lead the life of a hermit; he dwelt at first in a little house adjoining his cathedral, but finding that he was interrupted too often by visits that were not always motivated by piety, he dreamed, as he had dreamed earlier in Poitiers, of establishing for himself a more secluded retreat.

He eventually found this hermitage "about two miles from the city", that is to say, about the same distance away as Ligugé was from Poitiers. Indeed, he had noticed an out-of-the-way place almost surrounded by the meandering Loire River, while "on one side it was walled in by the rock-face of a high mountain." Thus, Sulpicius Severus tells us, this retreat was so remote that a hermitage in the wilderness would scarcely have been an improvement over it. It is easy to locate today, because the place in question later became the monastery of Marmoutier, around eight kilometers from Tours, and it has retained that name. The biographer explains that Martin built for himself a wooden cell, whereas most of those who gradually came to join him preferred to hollow a sort of caveman's dwelling out of the rock that loomed over the site—and such caves can be seen to this day. And, even more so than at Ligugé, a monastery was formed even before the term existed—let us say, before the Rule of Saint Benedict, which two hundred years later would be adopted by all those [in the West] who sought to lead a life of prayer in community.

According to the biographer, there were about eighty disciples there, and the chronicle portrays them as living the life of monks as that life would be commonly practiced later on throughout Christian Europe. No one owned any personal property; it was forbidden to buy or to sell; each one kept to his cell, although it is also noted that they gathered for communal prayer. They all took their meals together, "after the fast was ended"; that hour is not specified, and anyway it must have varied according to the liturgical seasons. No one drank wine, except for those who were ill, and the chronicle says that "most of them wore clothes of camel's hair." This is quite surprising; are we to assume that they had bolts of camel's hair material brought in from the East?

Another surprising statement: "No craft practised there except that of the copyist, and that was assigned to the younger men. The older ones were left free for prayer." We have not yet arrived, then, at the principle upon which the Rule of Saint Benedict would be founded: *Ora et labora*,

"Pray and work." This sheds light on how this precept might still, in Benedict's time, have seemed rather scandalous. For manual labor was the work of slaves; it was out of the question that a free man or an intellectual should work with his hands. And in fact, in the fourth century, in Martin's community, those who prayed did not work. It would be another two hundred years, almost, before Benedict's companions—all of them intellectuals who had studied in Rome or in Athens—could be led to consider that they would never be monks until they had personally put their hand to the plow. A momentous revolution in the history of humanity, if there ever was one!

We should note here extant proof of the work of the copyists of Marmoutier. The testimony is rather late, since it dates from the ninth century, that is, some five hundred years after Martin's death. The parchment in question is a manuscript of the Gospels of Lothair, executed between 849 and 851 (Latin MS no. 766 of the Bibliothèque Nationale in France). In it there is mention of a certain Sigibus, who says that by order of Lothair (half brother of Charles the Bald) he had this collection of Gospels made "in honor of Saint Martin, in the community of the saint, and entrusted to it as a testimony to the art [of calligraphy] cultivated there, so that he might be counted among the brothers and benefit from the prayers that the community would say for him, his wife, and his descendants". The woman in question, Lothair's wife, Hermingarde, died in 851, which implies that the Gospel book had been completed before that date. This notice proves the great renown and the extraordinary skill that continued to characterize the community of copyists at Marmoutier. A sacramentary of the same monastery has been preserved as well (now known as manuscript "no. 11-bis" of the Library in Autun), which was compiled at the command of Abbot Rainaud of Marmoutier around 851 and which includes three marvelous full-page illuminations.

The question arises, nevertheless: What was the livelihood of this community during the fourth century, since the work of the copyists was not enough to support it? It is true that the expenses for food must have been extremely modest. Perhaps, among those who had come to join the first companions of Martin, there were some men who owned a considerable fortune, as was the case with his own biographer, Sulpicius Severus. While distributing the proceeds from their properties, they could have kept some money for the support of their community, which had vowed to live a life of voluntary poverty. The chronicle explains that among those who had come to join Martin there were "a great number of noblemen".

It is quite moving to witness in this way the birth of the first religious congregations, the first monasteries—and to think of all those that soon after would be born and be scattered throughout Europe: the Benedictines of the early ages and those that would be produced by the subsequent reforms: the monks of Cluny and the Cistercians, who would soon give rise to a host of edifices—with all the splendor of Romanesque and Gothic art and architecture, to mention only those who are today the best and most widely known!

Those spiritual descendants, however, were still in the distant future, and the reader is struck by the impression of meekness, mutual understanding, and ready hospitality that emerges from the allusions that the chronicle of Sulpicius Severus makes to the community at Marmoutier. A little further on, in fact, he tells of how he himself went there, making a long journey in order to do so; he insists then on the kindness and humility with which he was welcomed. He relates how Martin invited him to share his meal and, to his great embarrassment, made it a point to bring him water with which to wash his hands. Furthermore, "in the evening, it was he who washed my feet. . . ." An atmosphere of charity permeated the place, where community life was practiced in a spontaneous sort of way, before there was any rule, which augured well for the communities that would develop later on. Martin began by instituting a reign of charity all around him.

Yet the monastery that was started at Marmoutier was no more a restful retreat for Martin than his episcopal see was. Actually, he was incessantly on the road—or, as we have remarked, on the country lanes—on the paths that led through woods and fields to clusters of dwellings. We have already noted this with regard to the pagan temples he destroyed and the trees and springs he dissuaded the peasants from venerating. And this hiking about would have a decisive influence on Christianity, which was still in its infancy there. Until then—and this was only normal in an empire where the town was the administrative unit and news center—it was in the towns that the bishops preached, celebrated the liturgy, and lived; surrounded by their staff of deacons and priests, they responded in this way to the essential needs in places where the people were gathered in large numbers. We have said it before: thanks to the ministry of the itinerant bishop that Martin turned out to be, the people of the *pagi* (in French, *pays*, from which comes the word "peasants") would cease to be *pagani*, pagans.

Martin preached in season and out of season; he addressed not only the crowds, but also smaller groups, and it was through his initiative that parishes sprang up. Even today tourists who travel through France are amazed to discover that it is practically impossible to find a village without its own steeple—a steeple that is a summit, but also a voice, a voice that calls and gathers and spreads news. We might reflect that, if each group of human habitations thus has its common voice, it is thanks to Martin's influence that this voice came about; he was one of the originators of the "parish" in the modern sense.[1] *Paroikia* is the Greek word for house, family, the domestic ties of a household, and the verb *paroikein* means "to dwell", "to live with". The Latin word *parochia* [from which is derived the French *paroisse*] is very close in meaning; this is a term that is frequently found in medieval documents. It could be said that, within the boundaries of the diocese, the parish sprang up at Martin's feet; he went about finding people where they lived so as to bring them to the one true God.

We find his footprints in Langeais, Saint-Pierre de Tournon, Ligueil, Sonnay, and Chisseaux—to speak only of the province of Touraine and the places that we are sure he has visited. But his peregrinations would take him much farther afield, beyond the limits of his diocese. It is astonishing to come across traces of his ministry, attested with certainty by an epitaph, as far away as Vienne in the province of Dauphiné. One inscription discovered by archeologists informs us that a certain woman named Foedula, upon entering that place, had been *fonte renata Dei*, "reborn at the fountain of God"—baptized—by the hand of Martin, who is described in the inscription as a chief of nobleman (*proceris*).

Gregory, who served as bishop of Tours in the sixth century and was originally from Auvergne, surely reported faithfully the travels of Martin, which were still remembered in that region. He relates how his predecessor had gone to pay his respects at the tomb of a Christian virgin named Vitalina

---

[1] In the early centuries of the Church, the term *paroikia* designated what is now called an urban diocese. As rural areas became Christianized, the word was then applied to a region within a diocese to which the bishop assigned one or more priests as his representative(s). (Based on an overview in *Lexikon für Theologie und Kirche*, "Pfarrei".)—TRANS.

in the market town of Arthonne, near Riom. He also relates that the dignitaries of Riom, hearing that Martin was about to arrive, had formed a veritable procession to meet him, which was enough to drive Martin away, since he dreaded pompous processions. It is likely that he also went to Clermont, and there is certain proof that he was in the Forez region, given the number of places where it is said that he caused a spring to gush forth or destroyed a pagan temple. Then, too, the "miracle of the pine tree" took place near Autun. There are likewise many local traditions that tell of his being in Burgundy: in Avallon, Sens, Beaune, and Dijon.

In Sens, a landowner, the prefect Auspicius, saw his estates ravaged on a regular basis by hailstorms that devastated his fields and those in the surrounding areas. Martin began to pray "and thoroughly delivered the region from the scourge". A church in honor of Saint Martin was later dedicated on the site of that miracle. There are also traditions concerning his travels in Franche-Comté and as far as French-speaking Switzerland. Furthermore, Gregory of Tours also relates that in the province of Saintogne, near the capital city of Saintes, he made a stream spring up for a woman who had brought him a glass of water. It is probable that he had to go to Bordeaux, where a council was held in which he would have taken part. Several place names—for instance, Le Roc-Saint-Martin near La Motte, or La Font-Saint-Martin near Doulezou, give further evidence of his travels; he is even said to have buried one of his disciples, named Romain, near Blaye. His entire life was a pilgrimage, with points of reference here and there, places where he must have stayed because of the miracles that he worked there.

Martin's ceaseless travels were punctuated by memorable deeds. For instance, a journey that he made to Chartres, which is related by a friend of Sulpicius named Gallus—

whom the chronicler often has reason to make fun of because, being a true inhabitant of Gaul, as his name indicates,
he is rather accustomed to living well, and the asceticism
practiced by Sulpicius sometimes frightens him! This man
Gallus, therefore, who brings us into the biographer's inner
circle, tells his story in the presence of several friends of
Sulpicius and of other people who gathered quickly when
they heard that an eyewitness was going to relate an anecdote
about Martin. Several monks arrive, whose names are mentioned: the priest Evagrius; Aper; Sabbatius; Agricola;
another priest, named Ætherius; a deacon, Calupio; and a
subdeacon, Amator. Finally there is the priest Aurelius, who
arrives last and out of breath, having come from afar. Gallus
says that he is going to tell them "something that happened
in the city of the Carnutes [Chartres]". We must note here
that the city of the Carnutes was from earliest antiquity a sort
of religious capital, even before the invasion of Gaul by the
Romans. The Druids would gather there every year; furthermore, that was where they used to settle conflicts among the
various Celtic peoples, who were always quick to quarrel.

We will let Gallus tell the story: "There was a father who
had a twelve-year-old daughter, dumb from birth. He brought
her to show to Martin, and to ask that the man of blessings,
through his favour with God, would set her free from her
impediment." Now Martin arrived accompanied by two bishops, Valentinus and Victricius, the latter being the bishop of
Rouen. He did not fail to defer at first, saying that it would be
better to speak to his two cons, who were much holier than
he. But they joined their requests to those of the father and
begged Martin to do what was asked of him.

> Then Martin delayed no longer—and he is equally to be
> admired for his manifestation of humility and for the prompt-
> ness of his kindly action. He ordered all the bystanders to be

sent away and then, with only the bishops and the girl's father present, he prostrated himself in prayer in his usual way. Next, he blessed a little oil with the formula used in exorcisms and then poured the consecrated liquid into the girl's mouth, holding her tongue with his fingers as he did so.

Nor did the effects of this act of power disappoint the holy man. He asked her the name of her father and she replied at once. Her father cried out with joy mingled with tears as he clasped Martin's knees, declaring to the astounded onlookers that that was the first word he had heard his daughter speak.

It is moving to recall this miracle that took place on the plain of Beauce, the future site of the famous Cathedral of Chartres, where vast crowds converge, particularly gatherings of students and of young people, and that Martin hallowed this place by the cure of a little girl who regained her voice.

Another striking cure was worked by Martin when he arrived in Paris:

Then again, at Paris he was passing through the city gates accompanied by a great crowd when, to everybody's horror, he kissed the pitiable face of a leper and gave him his blessing. The man was at once cleansed from all trace of his affliction, and coming to the cathedral the next day with a clear skin he gave thanks for his recovered health.

It is said that this cure of the leper took place at the site of the future town of Saint-Marcel, where in modern times an ancient Christian cemetery has been discovered, not far from the spot where the road to Melun crossed the Bièvre River at the ford, where the oldest city walls were located. Obviously one would be tempted to imagine that the bishop passed through the gate named Saint-Martin, but that gate, in its day, was just opposite the *pont au Change* [bridge at the Exchange], where the clock tower stands today, at the corner of the palace. So that it is difficult to determine precisely the place where it happened.

Another one of his journeys was memorialized by a dramatic incident. The journey in question was for business purposes, if one may say so: a pastoral visit. It very probably occurred in Clion, formerly known as Claudiomagus, located about seventy kilometers from Tours, within the boundaries of the land of the Bituriges or, in modern parlance, the people of Bourges. It is Gallus, again, who mentions the episode: "The Church there is famous for its holy monks and also for a glorious company of consecrated virgins." Therefore, when Martin was traveling through, he stayed in the sacristy of the church. The clergy of that locality had carefully prepared his quarters: "They had built a bed for him with a great quantity of straw." Sulpicius adds that they had made up a big fire under the concrete flooring, which was already crumbling and quite thin. The church had probably been erected over the site of ancient baths that were heated by an underground furnace [*hypocauste*].

In any case, Martin found the couch too luxurious; he had grown accustomed to lying down on the ground, on a "hair-shirt"—a coarse blanket. So he sent the straw mat packing, and it ended up right above the fire carefully prepared by the local clergy so that it would burn all night, keeping warm the sacristy where Martin would be sleeping. As was his custom, he fell asleep on the floor, exhausted by his fatiguing journey. Toward midnight, through the cracked pavement, the swirling fire ignited the dry straw of the mat. Martin, awakened with a start by this unexpected development, was taken aback by the danger of this crucial situation, but especially, as he explained later on, by the trap that the devil had set for him, and he did not have recourse to prayer as soon as he ought to have done. For in his desire to dash outside, he struggled violently for a long time with the bolt with which he had fastened the door. Then he felt he was surrounded by the fire, which was burning so fiercely that it was consuming the garments he wore.

Finally he came to his senses. Realizing that his salvation lay, not in escape, but in the Lord, he took up the buckler of faith and prayer, turned entirely to the Lord and remained prostrated in the midst of the flames. Then the power of God warded off the fire, and Martin remained in prayer in the middle of a circle of flames that did him no more harm. The monks who were standing outside the door while the fire was raging and crackling finally managed to force open the bolted door and draw Martin from the midst of the flames, thinking that he had been completely charred by such a lengthy inferno. Moreover, "I call Our Lord to witness to my words", Sulpicius said,

> Martin himself told me, and confessed it with sighs, that on this occasion he had been caught by the devil's wiles. That was why, when startled out of his sleep, he had not had the sense to think of meeting the danger with the prayer of faith. And so long as he tried, with mind distraught, to break out through the door, the fire was fierce all round him. But as soon as he had once more taken the Cross for his standard and prayer for his weapon, the flames in the centre had fallen back and he had felt them now as dew upon him, after they had been giving him the most cruel burns.

Gallus also told of how later on, after his departure, the consecrated virgins who lived in the town of Clion hurried to the sacristy and carefully collected the little bits of straw from the place where he had slept. He adds: "A few days later, one of them took part of the straw that she had collected in order to bring a blessing on herself and put it round the neck of a demoniac tormented by a deceiving spirit. Without a moment's delay, quicker than you could say the words, the demon was expelled and the person was cured."

It was on the road to Chartres, at an unnamed place, that Martin raised a third person from the dead. Gallus says that he had just walked through a very populous town, and that the crowd "consisted entirely of pagans", for no one in the town had ever met a Christian. But at the news that such a great man was traveling by, the whole countryside as far as eye could see was covered with a multitude of people who flocked from all directions. Martin sensed that he had to work a miracle, Gallus remarks; he describes the bishop trembling under the influence of the Holy Spirit and preaching the Word of God to the pagans "in inspired utterance". Meanwhile, a woman made her way through the crowd: her son had just died. With arms outstretched, she presented the lifeless body to Martin, saying, "We know that you are a friend of God; give me back my son, my only son." The whole crowd, he adds, joined its cries to the mother's request.

Martin knew that for the salvation of those who were present, who were awaiting and did not know the Messiah, he could obtain a miracle. He took the child's body into his arms and knelt down; when he had finished his prayer, he stood up and "restored a living baby to its mother". An uproar of shouting in the crowd: "They all came hurrying and crowding around the knees of the man of blessings, asking him in all sincerity to make them Christians. He lost no time in making them all catechumens, in the field, just as they were, by stretching out his hand over all of them together." And, turning to his friends, the monks who were accompanying him, he added that this was quite permissible, that "a field where martyrs had often won their crown was no unfitting place for making catechumens." This was the third time that Martin brought someone back to life.

Not all of his travels, however, were so beneficial. One day he was the victim of a strange misunderstanding. It was on the occasion of one of his pastoral visits. He had gone a little ahead of his companions when from the other direction "a government coach full of service men came along the highway". It was an encounter between the saint and the most formidable of government officials, the tax collectors, who in those days were accompanied by a military escort. Now, as it happened, Martin, with his rather unkempt appearance and the black cloak that fell to his ankles, frightened the mules that were drawing the carriage; they turned aside, upsetting the order in the harnessed team so that the tax collectors had to jump down to straighten things out. Some of them, infuriated, laid hands on Martin, the cause of the ruckus that had frightened the mules, and began to hit him with a staff and a whip. Martin remained silent and motionless; the others were even more annoyed when they saw that he did not react. When his companions arrived, they found their bishop "lying almost lifeless on the ground, all smeared with blood and with wounds all over his body". They immediately lifted him up, put him on his donkey, and made off with all haste.

The military men, having calmed down, went back to their carriage and commanded the mules to continue along the road. The drivers shouted and cracked the whip right and left, but in vain: the beasts would not budge from the spot. Then all the travelers who were in the carriage got up and tried to convince the mules with repeated lashings; they even took up tree branches and beat them with all their might, "but all this savagery achieved nothing whatever. [The mules] remained standing like statues in precisely the same place."

The tax collectors did not understand what was happening. It occurred to one of them to ask who that man was whom they had just mistreated at the same spot. "They made enquiries of some passers-by and learnt that it was Martin they had so cruelly flogged. Then at last the explanation was clear to everybody; they could not [ignore] the fact that it was the injury they had inflicted on that great man that was causing them to be detained." They dashed off, caught up with Martin and his little band, threw themselves on their knees, begged forgiveness, and implored permission to continue their journey. "They begged and prayed, therefore, that [Martin] would grant them pardon for their crime and give them power to go on." Martin, for his part, suspected what was going on and had previously told his confreres that the tax collectors who had treated him so brutally were stuck back there and would not be able to move. "But now he gently forgave them, giving them leave to proceed and restoring to them the use of their mules."

Most of the other journeys that Martin made were required by his meetings with the great men of the world, those who held political power. In doing so he played a role that would be incumbent upon bishops for the next two or three centuries. In a world where all authority was crumbling— including that of the military and the tax collectors, which we have just seen exercised so ruthlessly!—little by little the bishop became the one to whom the people had recourse.

To be sure, among those in authority there were some who were already Christians, and often they had a profound respect for Martin. One of them was the former prefect, Arborius, who liked to attend the Mass celebrated by the bishop of Tours; he confided to Gallus, the friend of Sulpicius, that one day "when Martin was offering the holy sacrifice he saw his hand covered with the most splendid jewels and that when his hand moved he heard the gems clashing as they struck against one another". This same man

Arborius, who according to Sulpicius was "a saintly and entirely faithful soul", relied one day on Martin's help in an
unusual form. His daughter was "wasting away from the
acute fevers of a quartan ague". Not knowing what else to do,
he placed upon her bosom a letter from Martin that had just
been brought to him. At that very moment, says the chronicler, "the fever left her". Arborius was so struck by the cure
that he took the initiative of offering his daughter to God and
consecrating her to perpetual virginity. He went to find Martin and to ask him to clothe her in the habit of virgins.

In the fourth century, as you see, the authority that a father
had over his daughter was still absolute, as Roman law understood it. In this case, the daughter probably agreed with the
decision, but Arborius' gesture was nevertheless that of a
paterfamilias [the head of a Roman household] bringing his
daughter to the vestal virgins. The situation would soon
change; various Church councils decreed that the vow of
virginity must come from the individual herself and not from
parental authority; the latter would not regain that full force
again until much later, in the sixteenth century, during the
classical period [in France]—precisely because of the return
to Roman law in that era.

The cure of a young girl also marked the arrival of Martin
in Trier, where he went to call on the emperor. No doubt it
was not the first time that he came to that city; we have
already suggested his probable stays there in the past. Now
we see him reporting to the palace of Emperor Valentinian
a short time after his consecration as a bishop. What petition
did he come to place before his imperial majesty? We know
nothing about the particulars, but Valentinian had decided
to refuse the request; indeed, he ordered the palace doors
to be closed against him. He was a harsh man with an arro-
gant disposition; furthermore, he had an Arian wife, "who

had turned him entirely against the holy man". Twice Martin pounded at the doors that had obstinately been closed against him, to use the expression of Gallus, who narrates the incident.

"Martin . . . resorted to his well-known weapons." He covered himself in ashes and, wrapped in a hair shirt, prayed night and day, fasting from both food and drink. And according to Gallus' account, "on the seventh day an angel appeared to him and ordered him to go confidently to the palace, where the imperial gates, though closed against him, would fly open of their own accord." Martin went to the palace: the doors were open, no one stopped him, and without any hindrance he made his way to the emperor. The latter, upon seeing him approach, became furious and asked why the guards had let him enter. The bishop drew closer, while the emperor was seated on his chair, and the two men remained that way for a moment in silence, when suddenly "the imperial chair was enveloped in flames." He stood up more quickly than he would have liked and thus found himself standing in Martin's presence. At that, his disposition became milder.

> And he embraced many times the man he had determined to humiliate and . . . he admitted that he had been conscious of the presence of divine power. Nor did he wait for Martin to proffer his requests before granting everything he asked. . . . [A]nd when eventually Martin was going away he made him many presents. All of these, however, the blessed man refused, ever careful to preserve his [monastic] poverty.

It was probably during another journey to Trier, several years later, that a miraculous cure took place. Indeed, in that city "there was a girl . . . who was suffering from such acute paralysis that for a long time she had been altogether without the use of her body." Her whole family was distraught and

expected her to die, when suddenly Martin's arrival was an-
nounced. The father of the girl ran to meet him. Now the
bishop had already gone into the church. Martin stood there,
surrounded by other bishops and numerous clerics; yet with
no regard for anyone else, the father ran up to him, sobbing,
and embraced his knees. "My daughter", he said, "is dying of
a disease of the most pitiable kind and—worse than death—is
alive only in her breathing; her body is already a corpse.
Please come to her and bless her. I am sure that you are the
one to make a cure." Martin, astonished and quite embarrassed, tried to excuse himself; the father, weeping openly,
insisted even more, and begged him to come visit his daughter, who was on the verge of death. Finally, at the advice of
the other bishops who were with him, Martin consented to
go with him. He went therefore to the house.

> A huge crowd was waiting at the street door to see what the
> servant of God would do. First he resorted to his usual weap-
> ons in cases of this kind and prostrated himself on the ground
> in prayer. Then, after looking at the sick girl, he asked to be
> given some oil. This he blessed, then poured the hallowed
> liquid, now a powerful remedy, into the girl's mouth. At once
> her voice came back to her. Then, at his touch, little by little
> each of her limbs began to recover its life. Finally, in the sight
> of all, she rose and stood firmly on her feet.

The account says no more about it, but we can suppose that
Martin then returned to the church, since later on, when he
went to the imperial palace, his reputation as a miracle
worker (which was already considerable) had preceded him.
Now, having arrived at the palace, he was received not only
by the emperor, but also by the empress. The wife of the
emperor Maximus was Christian. Here is Gallus' account:

> [The emperor] often sent for Martin, entertained him in the
> palace and showed the deepest respect for him. All their talk

together was of things present and things to come, of the glory of believers and the immortality of the saints; and all the time, by day and by night, the Empress hung upon Martin's lips. Indeed, she matched the woman in the Gospels by watering the feet of the holy man with her tears and wiping them with her hair.

However embarrassed he may have been, Martin could not escape from such signs of devotion.

She went so far as to beg her husband, the Emperor Maximus, to join with her in compelling Martin to allow her to send all the servants out and wait on him alone at table. Nor could the man of blessings be over-obstinate in his resistance. With her own hands the Empress made the modest preparations. It was she who placed Martin's stool and brought his table, poured out the water for his hands and served the meal she had cooked. It was she who, while he ate, stood at a little distance as servants are trained to do, motionless as if rooted to the ground, in everything exhibiting the meekness of a menial, the humble bearing of a maid. When he wished to drink, it was she who mixed the cup and she who presented it. When the meal was over, she collected the bread crumbs and the scraps, in her strong faith valuing these leavings above the dainties of the imperial table.

When Gallus was telling this story to Sulpicius and his friend Postumianus, the latter, being a man of his times, thought it appropriate to make a remark: "What becomes of the common belief that no woman ever approached close to Martin? Here is this Empress not only approaching him but even waiting on him." To which Gallus replied that the empress had resembled both Martha and Mary in the presence of the Lord: "Like Martha she served and like Mary she listened."

Not all of Martin's meetings with the powerful men of his

day went that smoothly! In other circumstances, the same
Maximus would learn that the bishop was quite capable of
confronting even a ruler when he was convinced that the
latter deserved a rebuke. And so, at a time when "many
bishops from various parts of the world had assembled to
meet the Emperor Maximus . . . [and] the foul fawning of all
of them upon the sovereign was much remarked", Martin
declined the emperor's invitation to dine with him, "saying
that he could not sit at table with a man who had robbed one
Emperor of his throne and another of his life." Maximus had
to make an effort to convince him, declaring that although he
had assumed the imperial power, he had done so because his
own soldiers had forced it upon him; besides, his adversaries
had fallen on the battlefield, and so he was not directly responsible for their deaths. Martin eventually was convinced
and accepted his invitation to dinner.

Therefore the festive banquet took place, with the emperor
surrounded by his relatives—his brother and his uncle—as
well as by illustrious personages such as the prefect and the
consul Evodius. As for Martin, he was accompanied by another priest, who was directed to a low place at the table,
while Martin reclined near the sovereign. We must picture
the meal as it took place in antiquity: the Romans ate while
reclining, whereas the Gauls had always taken their meals
seated. Yet the practice continued for a time, a throwback to
Roman customs, of reclining for meals.

Now Sulpicius Severus tells the story:

> Toward the middle of the meal a servant, in accordance with
> custom, brought a goblet to the Emperor. He ordered it to be
> given instead to our most holy Bishop and waited expectantly
> to receive it from the Bishop's own hands. But Martin, after
> drinking himself, passed the goblet to his priest, holding that
> no one had a better right to drink immediately after himself

and that it would not be honest of him to give precedence over the priest either to the Emperor or to those who ranked next to him.

This sort of impropriety struck those in attendance as surprising at first, if not scandalous, but soon "the news went all round the palace that Martin had done at the emperor's table what no other bishop would have done even when dining with the least of his magistrates." There could have been no better way of demonstrating the complete independence of a representative of the Church with regard to the great ones of this world.

Martin, moreover, had predicted to this same Maximus that, if he went on a military campaign to Italy, he would at first attack and conquer the emperor Valentinian, but that he would perish soon afterward. And that is what happened. Valentinian was put to rout by Maximus' armies, and then, about a year later, having succeeded in rallying his troops, he seizes Maximus outside the walls of Aquila and put him to death.

To return to the subject of the holy bishop's dealings with representatives of the temporal authority, we should also mention the episode of the "tyrant of Tours".

Sulpicius calls the personage in question Count Avitianus. We see here the use of a term that would become very widespread in the following centuries: a count, *comes, comitis, comitem,* meant "companion" and, by extension, "delegate". By the feudal period (that is, five or six centuries later), the word *count,* without losing the original sense of companion and therefore delegate, had acquired the force of a title of nobility. The word *duke* underwent a somewhat similar development: derived from the Latin word *dux,* which in Martin's day designated an army officer, this was a military term that eventually became a title of nobility.

At any rate, this Count Avitianus had a despicable reputation. When Sulpicius mentions him, he says right away that he was so cruel and bloodthirsty as to be barbaric. One day he entered the city of Tours followed by a line of men in chains—it is not known whether they were prisoners or men convicted under common law. For anyone acquainted with the severity of punishment during the Roman era, however, there was no doubt as to their fate. "He ordered a number of different tortures to be got ready for their execution and arranged for the dismal proceedings to be carried out before a terrorized city the next day."

Martin learned about it and immediately set out alone "for the brute's official residence". It was almost midnight: in the nocturnal silence everyone was asleep, all the doors were closed.

> Martin lay down across the . . . threshold. Avitianus all this time had been sunk in heavy sleep but now he was assailed by an angel who woke him with a blow. "The servant of God", said the angel, "is lying before your threshold—and you are still sleeping?" When he heard these words he leapt out of bed in great disturbance of mind. He summoned his slaves and called out to them in panic that Martin was at the gates and that they must go at once and unbar them, or it would be an insult to the servant of God.

The whole episode evidently took place at a time when Martin, being the bishop, was respected by all. Now the domestics checked the doors within the palace and, "laughing among themselves at their master for having been taken in by a dream", they returned and said that there was no one at the door; whereupon Avitianus, reassured, calmly went back to sleep.

"Presently, however, he was struck a still more violent blow and shouted out that Martin *was* standing at the gates and because of that he could get no peace for mind or body. And while the slaves were dawdling he himself went outside the gates. There, as he had expected, he found Martin."

Then, impressed by that silent power that could make itself felt through thick walls and bolted doors, he exclaimed, "There is no need for you to say anything. I know what you want; I can see what you have come for. Do go away now at once before the anger of heaven destroys me for this insult to you." Understanding what it was that Martin had come to the palace to request, he summoned his officers and ordered them to release all the prisoners. Sulpicius, who relates the incident in his *Dialogues*, goes on to describe the rejoicing throughout the city, once the people were delivered from the wrath of Avitianus.

Subsequently, the relations between Martin and Avitianus must have been more peaceful, because the latter's wife once sent a flask of oil with the request that Martin bless the contents; holy oil with which sick people were anointed was often used as a remedy in those days. As the story goes: "The glass flask that contained [the oil] was round, with a bulge in the middle and an elongated neck, but this projecting neck was not filled with liquid, because it is usual in filling such vessels to leave room at the top of the neck for a stopper."

Now the priest relating the anecdote testified that he saw the oil "increase when Martin blessed it, to such an extent that the additional quantity overflowed and ran down from the top of the neck in all directions." The same phenomenon was observed when the flask was brought to the lady of the house. "So much oil overflowed in the hands of the boy who was carrying it that all his clothes were covered with the liquid that escaped. [Yet] the mistress got the vessel back full to the very brim."

The mention of this episode of blessed oil overflowing its

container prompted Gallus, who was present, to tell of a similar incident. Another glass flask was full of oil that Martin had blessed; as it happened, "a house-boy, not knowing that the flask was there, unthinkingly pulled away a cloth that had been laid over it and the jar fell on the marble floor. Everyone was terrified to think that God's blessing had been lost, but the flask was found to be uninjured, as if it had fallen on to the softest feathers." One might conclude from this that Martin's blessing, once given, could not be lost.

To return to Avitianus: the narrator declares that that man, whose ferocity was well known, behaved in a humane way only when he was in Tours; he recalls another incident: "I remember one day Martin going to visit him; and, when he had entered his private office, he saw sitting behind his back a demon of astonishing size. From where he was . . . Martin blew at it." Avitianus was surprised, thinking that the bishop was blowing at him. He asked Martin, "Why, holy man, do you behave [toward] me like this?" He replied: "It is not at you, but at him, that loathsome creature mounted on your shoulders." And the narrator adds: "It is certainly the case that from that day onwards Avitianus was more gentle, either because he now realized that he had always been the tool of the devil that was riding him, or because the evil spirit, once driven from its seat on him by Martin, was deprived of its power for mischief."

Again and again his contemporaries would find Martin battling against the demon.

6

The Community

In Martin's own community, things were not that simple. Certainly there were all those disciples who gathered around him so as to benefit from his teachings and to follow his example—those were the ones, both at Marmoutier and at Ligugé, who eventually formed a veritable monastery before the term existed, a prototype of those monastic legions that would populate the long centuries of feudal society.

But that does not mean that he himself never encountered difficulties among his close collaborators, as is evident from the almost comic story of his archdeacon in Tours. The man's name has not been handed down to us, but the episode is worth retelling, as Gallus does in one of the *Dialogues*,[1] especially considering that his account is quite charming and it is related with his special brand of humor. Gallus himself witnessed the incident: "This happened when I first went to live under the man of blessings after leaving college." Gallus was therefore still rather young. "Only a few days after that, we were accompanying him to the church and a beggar met him, half-naked, though it was in the winter, and asked to be given some clothing. The bishop called for his senior deacon and

[1] Reprinted in the anthology *The Western Fathers: Being the Lives of SS. Martin of Tours, Ambrose, Augustine of Hippo, Honoratus of Arles and Germanus of Auxerre*, trans. and ed. by F. R. Hoare (New York: Sheed & Ward, 1954).

ordered him to find a garment for the shivering creature without delay. Then he went into the sacristy and sat there alone, as his custom was."

Gallus tells us something about Martin's habits: he usually spent a few moments alone before praying the Divine Office; he would let the priests who accompanied him deal with anyone who asked for him, while he himself remained in seclusion in the sacristy. While he is on the subject, Gallus remarks that he never saw Martin seated in a real chair and that he was content to sit on one of those rustic three-legged stools "which we Gauls call *tabourets* but you learned people, or at least you, Postumianus, who have been in Greece, would call tripods." He stresses this detail, recalling how other bishops had a taste for raised platforms. "[I once saw] a certain person sitting upon a lofty throne raised high upon a kind of royal dais."

On that day, Blessed Martin's solitude was disturbed. The beggar in question, seeing that the archdeacon was taking his time about giving him a tunic, burst into the sacristy in tears, complaining that the cleric had forgotten him and shouting that he was cold. "Without a moment's delay the holy man stealthily slipped off his tunic from under his vestment without the beggar seeing, put it on him and told him to be off."

Meanwhile the archdeacon arrived: the Divine Office was about to begin, the people were waiting in the church; it was time for Martin to go out into the sanctuary. Martin then replied that he had to clothe the beggar first: this time he was speaking about himself! The archdeacon did not understand; he did not notice that the bishop no longer had his tunic on under his surplice, and that it would not be decent for him to show himself in public. The archdeacon therefore, by way of excusing his own negligence, said that the beggar had disappeared. "Well, then," Martin replied, "let the garment which has been found for him be brought to me. There will be a beggar waiting to wear it."

The cleric, infuriated, ran from the church to the nearest shop, selected what the text of the *Dialogues* calls a "bigerrica", which was a shaggy woolen tunic [worn by the inhabitants of Bigorre in the Pyrenees], paid five pieces of silver, brought it back and threw it at Martin's feet, saying, "There's your garment but there's no beggar here."

Martin, quite unmoved, ordered the archdeacon to wait for him a moment outside the door—giving him time to put a tunic back on under his surplice. Gallus notes that he made every effort to keep what he had done a secret. . . . And vested in that way, he went out into the church to offer a sacrifice of praise to God.

On that day Gallus claims to have seen, at the moment when Martin blessed the altar, "a ball of fire dart out from his head, so that, as it rose in the air, the flame drew out into a hair of enormous length. And although we saw this happen on a great festival in front of a huge congregation, only one of the nuns, one of the priests and three monks saw it."

Another anecdote from the inner circle concerns Clarus and Anatolius. The former, Clarus, was a high-ranking nobleman in Martin's community, probably at Marmoutier. He had been ordained a priest; he was dead at the time that Sulpicius, in his *Life of Saint Martin*, tells the story. A young man by the name of Anatolius had come to see him, saying that he, too, wanted to lead a monastic life, to live with him and the other brothers. This Anatolius, to all outward appearances, was a humble and righteous man. But after a time he declared that angels came quite often to converse with him. At first no one believed him, but little by little he grew more convincing, claiming that he received messages from the Lord and that he should be considered a prophet. Clarus, however, absolutely refused to be taken in; Anatolius threatened him with the wrath of God and finally exclaimed, "I tell you, this very night God will give me a shining robe from out of heaven and I will make my abode among you clad in it, and it shall be a sign to you that in me dwells the Power of God, who has presented me with His garment."

The brothers, impressed by this statement, waited for the promised sign to be given them. And indeed, around midnight some sounds were heard.

> You could see, too, the cell which housed this young man ablaze with a mass of lights; and there was heard the thudding of feet running about in it, and what might have been the murmur of many voices. Then came silence and he emerged and called one of the brethren, named Sabatius, and showed him the tunic he was wearing. The brother in amazement called the rest to come, and even Clarus came hurrying up. A light was brought and all carefully inspected the garment. It was exceedingly soft, with a surpassing lustre, and of a brilliant [whiteness], but it was impossible to tell the nature of the material. At the same time, under the most exact scrutiny of eyes and fingers it seemed to be a garment and nothing else.
>
> Meanwhile Clarus had been urging the brethren to pray their hardest to be shown by the Lord what it was. The rest of the night, therefore, was spent in singing hymns and psalms.
>
> At daybreak he took Anatolius by the hand with the intention of taking him to Martin, being well aware that Martin could not be taken in by a trick of the devil. At this, the wretched man began to resist and protest loudly, saying that he had been forbidden to show himself to Martin. And when he was being forced to go against his will, between the hands of those who were dragging him the garment disappeared.

In other words, whether diabolical or not, it was an illusion, but one that could not have fooled the bishop of Tours. Sulpicius, in relating this story, compares this deception by Anatolius with several other contemporary events: for instance, a young man in Spain who claimed to be Elijah, who went so far as to say that he was the Christ. Whereupon a bishop, named Rufus, who had been completely taken in by the hoax, rendered him homage, so that Rufus was deposed by the other bishops. Similar individuals who have managed to deceive others have appeared over the centuries. Sulpicius sees in this the coming of the false prophets predicted in the Apocalypse of John [Revelation]. In our time, we could point to gurus or marabouts, who do not hesitate to claim all sorts of honors in the sects that are so numerous in our own century.

Within his own inner circle, moreover, Martin had to put up with instances, if not of rebellion, then at least of ill humor that were sometimes serious! In particular, the moods of his young companion whom the chronicles call Brictio or Brice, who later succeeded him in the episcopal see of Tours. In his youth he experienced bouts of anger against the bishop, and Martin was convinced that they were stirred up by the devil. One day the bishop was sitting as usual on his wooden stool in a little courtyard surrounding his cell in Marmoutier, when he saw two demons struggling on the cliff that loomed over the monastery. They were calling, "Come on, Brice; come on, Brice," in what the text of the *Dialogues* calls "eager, gleeful tones". They saw Brice approaching from a distance and knew what sort of rage they had aroused in him.

"Nor, indeed, was there any delay before Brice burst in raging and, then and there, like a raving lunatic, spat out a thousand insults against Martin. For he had been reprimanded by him the day before." Before entering the clergy, Brice had never owned anything; he had even been fed at the monastery through Martin's charity. Now he was raising horses, buying slaves, and, as the text notes, "it was being freely said of him . . . that it was not only boys of barbarian stock that he bought, but also girls with pretty faces." Accusations of this sort had driven him mad with anger, and now he raged against Martin so violently that he almost came to blows. Martin, however, with a placid expression on his face, remained calm; he tried to pacify Brice and speak kindly to him, but the latter, "with trembling lips and unsteady countenance, and white with fury", hurled insults and replied to the accusations made against him by boasting that he was holier than all of them. *He* had grown up at the monastery, raised by Martin himself, while "Martin, on the other hand, at the beginning of his career had been soiled, as he could not deny, by the life of a soldier; and now, at the end of it, as the result of baseless superstitions . . . , had completely sunk into his dotage."

While still spewing forth insults, Brice went away. Suddenly, in the middle of the road along which he had arrived, he stopped; the narrator attributes this to Martin's prayer and to the fact that the demons had been driven from his soul, leaving room for repentance. "Before long he had returned to Martin and was prostrate at his knees. He begged for pardon, he acknowledged that he had been wrong and, now that he was at last comparatively sane, he admitted that a demon had been at work in him." Martin, who remained as calm and peaceful as before, told him how he had seen the demons antagonizing the priest, and consequently had not been bothered at all by the hail of insults.

This Brice certainly was not easy to get along with. Sulpicius relates that he was even brought before the diocesan tribunal for several misdeeds, which he does not specify.

When someone complained of him to Martin, he replied, "If Christ put up with Judas, why should not I put up with Brice?" And from Martin's example Sulpicius concludes that one should reply patiently to anyone who is angry: patience and serenity make it possible to conquer anger and experience forgiveness.

The story leads us to consider Martin in his battle with the devil, a subject that comes up more than once in his life. Although in certain instances, like that of Brice, we might think that speaking of demons is a metaphorical way of describing the fits of anger of a man who is beside himself, in other cases a presence is clearly mentioned and described. Thus, one day when Martin was at prayer, a luminous figure appeared to him, in royal garb, "crowned with a diadem of gems and gold, and gold gleamed upon his shoes. His face was serene and his expression joyful." Martin left off praying in astonishment. For a long time each one remained silent, then the apparition began to speak: "Martin, you see me. Acknowledge me. I am Christ. I am about to come down upon the earth and I wished first to manifest myself to you." Martin kept silent and the apparition repeated his statement: "Martin, why so slow to believe, now that you see? I am Christ."

Martin made an unexpected reply: "The Lord Jesus did not say that he would come in purple robe and glittering diadem. I will only believe in a Christ who comes in the garments and the lineaments of His Passion, who comes bearing upon Him the wounds of the Cross." At that, the apparition vanished, dissolving like smoke and leaving behind in the cell "such a stench as to put it beyond doubt that it was the devil indeed".

And Sulpicius notes that he heard of this incident from the lips of Martin himself, "lest anyone think that I am romancing".

Another even more dramatic incident: "Once [the devil] burst into his cell with a tremendous clatter, holding in his hand a blood-stained ox-horn. Fresh from committing crime, he displayed his right hand covered with blood. 'Martin,' he said gleefully, 'where is your power? I have just killed one of your people.'" Sulpicius continues the account:

> Martin thereupon called the brethren together and told them what the devil had revealed and ordered them to go carefully through all the cells to see who had been the victim of the tragedy. They reported that none of the monks was missing but that a rustic hired to cart wood was gone into the forest. He told some of them, therefore, to go and meet him. Thus he was found not far from the monastery, already almost lifeless. But, though at his last gasp, he made it plain to the brethren how he came by his mortal wound. He was tightening up some thongs that had got loose on his team of oxen when an ox had tossed its head and dug a horn into his groin. And before long he was dead.

Not all of the demonic manifestations were so dramatic, but Martin had to ward them off repeatedly, and in doing so used only one weapon: the Sign of the Cross and prayer. Certain monks testified that they had heard the devil reproaching Martin for having admitted to the monastery, after their conversion, "certain brethren who had lost the grace of baptism by various misdeeds—and [the devil] specified the crimes of each. Martin had defended himself against the devil most firmly, saying that former offences could be wiped out by leading a better life and that the Lord in His mercy had ordained that absolution from their sins was to be given to those who had left off sinning."

When the devil retorted that a guilty man remains guilty, Martin exclaimed, "If you yourself, wretched being, would cease to prey upon mankind and would even now repent of your misdeeds, now that the Day of Judgment is at hand, I have such trust in the Lord Jesus Christ that I would promise you mercy."

It would be difficult, indeed, to extend the meaning of forgiveness any farther than that!

Such direct dealings with the devil, the being who is negation itself, might appear in our day to be legends made out of whole cloth and devoid of truth. Not so long ago, however, another saint, Jean-Marie Vianney (who died in 1859 and was canonized in 1925), is said to have experienced likewise the attacks of the devil, whom he called "*le grappin*" [roughly, "Old Scratch"], who used to taunt and maltreat him, without intimidating him, though.

Be that as it may, and taking into account that fact that the hostile attitude of such conversation partners is often attributed to the devil by a sort of literary stylistic device, Martin's favorite weapon against this negative living thing was the Sign of the Cross—which scholars have determined had been in use since the beginning of the fourth century. This Christian gesture was only belatedly introduced, but the peace that came over the Church with the end of the persecutions and the discovery of the Cross of Christ by Saint Helena made it into the characteristic sign of a Christian.

7

Women

Women did not play much of a role in Martin's life; you may recall those whom he cured, such as the girl in Trier, but all in all he is a man of his time insofar as he maintained the distance between man and woman that was customary in antiquity. To be sure, there were women martyrs whom the Church has raised to the honor of the altars—which was quite an amazing development for the society of that day, especially in the case of martyrs who, like Blandina, were simple slaves who could be treated as things and not as persons. Yet even though there were, from the very beginning, more women saints than men, it was only gradually, with the passage of time, that women assumed a more important place in the Church; the Virgin Mary was not really discussed until the following [i.e., fifth] century, and in 431, at the Third Ecumenical Council of Ephesus, the Blessed Virgin was declared the Mother of God, *Theotokos*—a title that certain Churches in the East would not accept. In Martin's day no one could have foreseen the double monasteries of the seventh century, in which monks and nuns—while living, of course, in separate buildings and meeting only in church—would be under the authority of an abbess and not of an abbot. Some three centuries would have passed meanwhile, and it would take that long for the presence of women to assert itself in a society from which, through all of antiquity, they had been banished and in which they had been regarded merely as sex objects.

There is a revealing story, recorded by Sulpicius in his *Dialogues*, in which we see Saint Martin learning a lesson in austerity from a woman religious and being pleased about it. We will let Gallus recount the incident:

> I expect, Sulpicius, that you remember (because you were present yourself) the deep feeling with which Martin sang the praises of the consecrated virgin who had withdrawn so completely from the sight of any man whatever that she would not even receive Martin when he wished to pay her the compliment of a visit. He was passing near the little property where she had lived for many years in chaste seclusion and, having heard of her fidelity and her virtues, he turned aside there with the idea that, by this pious act of courtesy performed in his capacity as Bishop, he could do honour to a virgin of such outstanding worth.
>
> We who were with him had supposed that when a Bishop of such renown modified the strictness of his own rule of life so far as to come and see her, the virgin would be delighted at receiving this recognition of her virtues. But she would not loosen the fetters of her heroic rule even for a sight of Martin. Apologies that were wholly to her credit were sent out to him through another woman and the man of blessings turned joyfully away from the doors of one who had not allowed him to see or greet her.

And so, far from being offended by her refusal or considering it as an affront, Martin simply praised the virtue of that woman who, having consecrated herself to God many years previously, turned down his visit.

Gallus then continues his account:

Well, when night came on and we were obliged to stop not far from her little estate, she [the same virgin] sent a gift to the man of blessings as to a guest. And Martin did a thing he had never done before, for [ordinarily] he would accept no parting gift nor any present from anyone. [But this time] he returned not one of the articles which the revered virgin had sent him. It was certainly not for a bishop, said he, to reject a benefaction from one who should be esteemed above many bishops.

And Gallus points out the moral of the story, the only one that occurred to him in his day: "I trust that all consecrated virgins will take note of that example. If they wish their doors to be closed against evil men, they must shut them even against good men." As far as he was concerned, it was impossible to go too far in practicing mutual reserve. Several of his reflections on the strangeness of the case follow:

A virgin would not let herself be seen by Martin! It was certainly no common-or-garden[-variety] bishop that she repelled. The man to whom the virgin would not show herself was one whom it was a saving grace to see. And what bishops besides Martin would not have regarded it as an affront? Think of the irritation, think of the angry feelings that would have been aroused in his mind against the holy virgin! He would have pronounced her a heretic and decreed her excommunication. More acceptable to him than that chosen soul would have been those virgins who are always contriving to be where they will meet the bishop and who give expensive banquets at which they even sit with him at table!

He ends his diatribe by adding: "When I praise in this way the virtues of this particular virgin, I do not want to be thought to be criticising the many who came long distances to see Martin." And he compares them to the angels who often hastened in the same way to pay a visit to blessed Martin.

It is evident from this how much mutual mistrust still prevailed between men and women. And there is nothing surprising about that in a society that had scarcely managed to free itself from the customs of the ancient world. In the era when Sulpicius and Gallus were conversing, the Roman Senate had still not forbidden the killing of newborn girls, which was common during Roman antiquity. The contemporary treatises on family law euphemistically call this practice the forced disappearance [*la disparition forcée*] of younger daughters—since it was, in general, the oldest daughter who was kept for the purpose of procreating, whereas the younger daughters were "suppressed". We shouldn't be too quick to protest: in our own century, many people are stunned to learn that in certain Asian countries it has become common to allow the second or third daughter born into a family to die, whereas in places like China, where by order of the state a family must limit itself to only one child (!), many mothers make sure that the only child kept is a boy. . . . And scientific progress, in the form of ultrasound, enables them to make such a monstrous choice! This suffices to show how much progress remains to be made, even in our modern societies, in order for men and women to be treated with equal dignity, according to the teaching of the Bible, as creatures of God.

In Martin's day, although Christians were famous for keeping all of their children, whether daughters or sons, and although many women were honored as saints and invoked in prayer, even at the altars during the Liturgy of the Eucharist—something that surely amazed some of the new converts!—there was still a certain mistrust toward women, even on the part of Christians. Woman was still the one who led others into sin; it was safer, for her as well as for everyone else, believers or not, if she remained cloistered, unseen. Furthermore, it is curious to see this sentiment reemerging in the sixteenth century; in that era, as we have noted, [the Church in France] forbade the foundation of religious communities for women unless they were cloistered. Even the Order of the Visitation Sisters, which was originally supposed to work among the poor and "visit" them, was approved only on the condition that it become an order of cloistered nuns. And it is well known how Saint Vincent de Paul, when he founded the Daughters of Charity, took great care to explain to them that they were not women religious and that they should not wear the veil, which would have inevitably resulted in their being cloistered, whereas he insisted that they assume the duty of visiting the poor, which was a crying need at that time, going into any neighborhood whatsoever in order to relieve the misery of the people—which had become so distressing in the seventeenth century.

It was not until the age of feudalism that a woman could enjoy true equality with a man; that is to say, that men and women—each sex according to its nature and maintaining its identity in a genuinely equitable society—would have equal but different rights, as is only normal. As a result, a queen could reign and did reign alone if her husband was absent or if he had died. The Order of Fontevraud, which, at the beginning of the twelfth century, revived an institution that had already existed since the seventh century, namely, double monasteries headed by an abbess rather than an abbot, became characteristic of civilized society, understood and put into practice in this way.

In Martin's day, strict separation between men and women was the rule in religious communities; an example is the old soldier who

> had laid aside his sword-belt in the church and entered upon the monastic life. His wife, for her part, had entered a convent. But the gallant hermit went to Martin, saying that he

should have his wife live with him, without giving up his habit or his eremitic life; that they would not return to their conjugal ways, "that all he wanted was the comfort of his wife's company".

To all this Martin replied . . . : "Tell me, were you ever on active service and have you ever fought in the front line?"

"I have often fought in the front line," [the soldier] replied, "and I was often on active service."

"Then tell me", said Martin, "when weapons were ready and the line was being marshalled for battle, or when contact had been made, swords were drawn and actual fighting was going on with the enemy, did you ever see a woman standing or fighting in the line?"

Then the soldier was at last abashed. He blushed, and then thanked Martin for not letting him continue in his mistake and particularly for putting him right by a sound and reasoned analogy instead of by a harsh reproof.

And Martin explained to his companions:

A woman should not come near the men's lines. The fighting formations should be kept quite separate and the women should live in their own quarters, far away. It makes an army ridiculous if a troop of women invades the men's battalions. A soldier's place is fighting in the line and on the battle-field; a woman should keep behind the fortifications. She can win glory too, by living chastely while her husband is away. For her, the first virtue and the crowning victory is that she should not be seen.

Although this conclusion seems to us today excessively strict, it is in any case quite appropriate to the times and the situation then: Martin himself had been a soldier, and he knew what an army in battle array was.

Furthermore, nothing prevents us from formulating a more general moral to the story. Indeed, a woman is not interested in war; she knows better than a man does the price

of peace. The female personality itself includes a certain horror of war, and we might wonder—at the end of the twentieth century, which seems to have been devoted to a perpetual
war, from Sarajevo in 1914 to Sarajevo in 1995, that has
increasingly overwhelmed the civilian populations—whether
someday women won't be more conscientious about this
deep-seated evil.[1] What would happen if they were better
represented and held more influential positions in the international organizations that claim to be opposed to war, from
the U.N. to NATO? Until now they have not played a very
prominent role. Could this be the great hope that should be
held out for the twenty-first century, that more women will
be involved and therefore will have a chance to be more
effective? Who knows whether women might not be better
than males at finding paths to peace? It would be worth a try.

The fact remains that, in Martin's time, the state of virginity or celibacy practiced for the love of Christ involved over-
coming living habits and a view of society that had been
foundational for centuries. The whole question is somewhat
similar to that of slavery, which still seemed completely natural in the fourth century, even though the Church's councils
were already excommunicating anyone who killed a slave he
owned.

We can conclude this same line of thought with a comparison that Martin made while walking over a meadow with
his monks:

> Oxen had been grazing down part of a certain meadow and
> another part of it had been rooted up by swine. The rest had
> not been touched and was rich with verdure and painted with
> flowers of many colours. "That part there," [Martin] said,
> "where the cattle have been feeding, is a good representation

---

[1] Régine Pernoud was writing this book in 1995.— ED.

of marriage. It has not altogether lost the beauty of the grass but has not kept any of the glory of the flowers. That part which the pigs—those unclean creatures—have rooted up makes a loathsome picture of fornication. But that part there, which has not been injured at all, shows us the splendour of virginity. It is rich with abundant grass, it will give a luxuriant crop of hay, and it is beautiful beyond comparison, decked out with flowers and shining as if adorned with sparkling gems. A sight most blessed, a sight worthy of God! For nothing can compare with perfect chastity."

And he went on denouncing the error of the heretics who compared marriage to fornication, as well as the error of those who placed marriage on the same level as virginity. He concluded: "Marriage may be pardoned, virginity looks towards heavenly glory, and fornication is destined to punishment unless it is purged by penance."

In our time, no doubt, we are more sensitive to the idea of being called to a particular state in life; we would emphasize the vocation to marriage, which is no less important than the vocation to the life of consecrated religious.

The importance of virginity was thoroughly understood and acknowledged during the centuries that we call the Middle Ages. And Mary's virginity was not called into question. Nowadays it is almost amusing to read the objections voiced here and there by some authors who bring up in this regard the "brethren of Jesus" who, indeed, are mentioned several times in the Gospels (Mt 12:46; Mk 3:31–35; Jn 2:12, 7:3–10). They overlook the fact that the Greek language has only one word, *adelphos*, with which to designate brother, relative, or cousin;[2] it is difficult to see how else the evangelists could have referred to the sons and daughters of Mary's

---

[2] At the very most, the term *exadelphos* was used to designate specifically what we refer to as a cousin (although etymologically it meant "nephew").

siblings or of Joseph's! In those days people were not always concerned about differentiating the members of the extended family. It evidently sufficed, in earlier centuries, to recall what may have been the last thing that Jesus said to his mother: "Woman, behold *your* son", before his death on the Cross (Jn 19:26). But today the focus is on the sexual act rather than on the sense of family and what that implies.

It is striking to note that, in the sixteenth century, with the return of Roman law in [Western European] intellectual history and the legalism that it imposed upon society, the situation of women once again became very much like what it was in the ancient world: strictly subject to the father's guardianship at first, and then to that of the husband; and this trend became more and more pronounced [in France] until the nineteenth century, with the Civil Code, in which women are not mentioned, just as they were absent from both public and private law during the Roman era. It was not until the twentieth century, to a large extent through the influence of external circumstances (the incessant wars, etc.), that women little by little regained, despite the Civil Code, several rights to act as individual persons, and especially to choose freely how they would act.

We might note in this regard that the evolution of the status of women, curiously enough, followed an arc that ran parallel to that of the institution of slavery. For, strange to say, in an era that claimed to be Christian, slavery paradoxically reemerged also in the sixteenth century. And it did not disappear from French law until 1848—and much later in other countries, such as Brazil.

In the meantime—and we insist on this fact—slavery had completely vanished in Christian Europe. From the fourth century on, slaves were emancipated *en masse*. The emancipation movement kept spreading, and by the mid-seventh century, when Queen Bathilde prohibited the last slave markets in her kingdom, there were practically no slaves left in Europe. Serfdom, which some have tried to equate with slavery, is radically different from it, in that the serf is considered to be a person, and not a thing: he has the right to a family, and the tenure that is granted to him on the lord's domain cannot be taken from him, and it passes on to his family after his death. In the thirteenth century, Philippe de Beaumanoir could write: "No one in this kingdom is a slave." Nobody could have suspected then that slavery would be reintroduced at the height of Christian civilization, in the sixteenth century, in the American colonies, and that it would be practiced in good conscience for several centuries by various shipowners, merchants, and colonists who belonged to "Christian" families!

8

The Priscillian Affair

In the life of Martin there was an episode that left a profound impression on him, and he himself admitted that he had some difficulty in recovering from it. It was a very typical episode, since it can be viewed as a preliminary version of or, in any case, an attempt at what would someday be the Inquisition: the spiritual authority having recourse to the temporal authority in the hopes that it would help to get rid of a heresy and to subdue those who spread it. Resorting, in other words, to an "easy" solution, which was often tried in that period when heresies were multiplying, but which Martin wanted to avoid. We are talking about the Priscillian affair, which caused a lot of ink to be spilt in its day, and again in our time, since previously unknown documents on this subject were discovered and edited in 1889.

Priscillian, a Spaniard of noble birth who was wealthy and well educated, had begun to spread doctrines infected with Gnostic and Manichean errors, against the background of magical practices to which he had been addicted, some said, ever since his youth. He had a following of faithful enthusiasts, both men and women, and was very highly regarded by certain bishops: he himself was appointed bishop of Avila. As Priscillian explained it, the human soul was a particle of the divine substance; according to his teaching, which was tinged with a sort of astrological fatalism, souls that were instructed by angels had to pass through certain circles where they would be made subject to the powers of evil and end up in one body or another, in which they had to suffer the effects of a sentence that Christ would one day overturn by nailing it to the Cross. He cited the Gospel parable of the sower, teaching that this sower assigned men to bodies of his choosing.

With all this astrological and philosophical folderol, Priscillian denied the Holy Trinity; he saw the soul as a particle of God that had fallen into the material world, and he regarded creation as a sort of prison in which guilty men expiated their crimes. We should add that Priscillian strictly ordered his followers to disclose only one part of their doctrine. He is quoted as having commanded them to "swear, perjure yourselves, but guard your secret at all costs." That is to say, they had to make sure not to reveal to ordinary, carnal men the spiritual sense [of their doctrines], which was accessible only to the initiated. Some writers traced the heresy of the Priscillianists back to the teachings of Simon the Magician, who is mentioned in Scripture [Acts 8].

Priscillian and his disciples, among them several women, caused much trouble in Spain; they were accused of misconduct or, perhaps, of performing obscene rituals. In any case a council that was convened in Saragossa in 380, consisting of about a dozen bishops, stigmatized the errors of Priscillian and declared that he was suspected of heresy; at the same time two bishops, Instantius and Salvianus, supported him. In response to the council, these two bishops hastened to appoint Priscillian to the see of Avila (he was still a layman). Two other bishops who had participated in the Council of Saragossa, Bishop Hydatius of Mérida and Bishop Ithacus of Ossonuba, were assigned to notify him of the sentence of excommunication.

Now the last-named bishops thought it opportune to call upon the secular authorities, to wit, Emperor Gratian, in order to drive the heretics from their dioceses; they were in fact banished and forbidden to stay anywhere within a hundred miles of their former sees. As soon as the three bishops— Instantius, Salvianus, and Priscillian—were condemned, they decided to go to Rome to bring their case before Pope Damasus. They traveled through the province of Aquitaine and were well received in the town of Eauze, where they won some new disciples over to their doctrine; on the other hand, the bishop of Bordeaux, whose name was Delphinus, shut the door in their face. They were welcomed on the estate of a woman called Euchrotia, who decided to join the group, along with her daughter, Procula. The latter would eventually be accused of having illicit relations with Priscillian; indeed, after finding that she was with child, she had recourse to various contrivances in order to terminate her pregnancy.

The little band arrived at Rome, where Pope Damasus categorically refused to grant them an audience. Thereupon one of the bishops, Salvianus, died. The others, on the trip back, tried to get Bishop Ambrose to welcome them to Milan. But he, like Damasus, would not open his doors to them. They won an imperial agent over to their side; this was the palace official [*maître des offices*], an important man named Macedonius. He delivered to them a rescript that permitted them to return to their respective dioceses in Spain, and he commended them to the pro-consul of Spain, one Volventius. So there they were, back in their country, completely free; they even gave the impression of being victorious. Now the bishop of Ossonuba, Ithacus, found that it was his turn to be persecuted; he had to flee to Gaul; he tried to appeal to the emperor, but Macedonius was monitoring written communications; Ithacus fled as far as Trier. This took place in the year 382.

Thereupon a military revolution broke out: the armies stationed in Trier named Maximus the new emperor—he was also a Spaniard and an old standby of Theodosius, emperor of the East. When Maximus made his entrance into Trier, Ithacus, who had taken refuge with Brito, bishop of Trier, managed to get a good reception and to warn him against Priscillian and his sect. As a result, the prefect of the Gaulish territories and the emperor's vice-regent in Spain received orders to arrest Instantius and Priscillian and to bring them to Bordeaux to be judged by a council there.

Instantius was the first to be interrogated, and he did not succeed in convincing the judges; he was declared deposed from his episcopal see. Priscillian, feeling that he himself was threatened, decided to appeal the case to the emperor.

At this point we will let Sulpicius Severus continue the story, as he relates it in his *Chronicle* [Book II, chapters 49–50].[1]

> Priscillian, unwilling to appear before the bishops [of the Council of Bordeaux], appealed from them to the emperor [Magnus Maximus]. This appeal was made possible by the wavering of our bishops: they ought to have pronounced their sentence, even against someone who was in contempt of court, or else, if they themselves were suspect, they ought to have referred the matter to other bishops, but they should not have allowed a case of this sort, in which the crimes were so manifest, to go to the Emperor.

It is encouraging for us to see Sulpicius Severus speaking out in this way against the fact that religious figures, in a matter concerning heresy, went to the temporal authorities. This is always a dangerous temptation, which has deplorable results, like the repeated exiles of an Athanasius. Then, too,

---

[1] The passages from the *Chronicle* of Sulpicius Severus were translated from the French.—TRANS.

the Priscillian affair, as remote as it might seem, deserves to be studied centuries later, and Sulpicius Severus is perfectly aware of this, as was Martin himself. The *Chronicle* continues:

> Thus all who were involved in the affair were brought before the Emperor. They were followed by their accusers, Bishops Hydatius and Ithacus. I would not blame their zeal to condemn heretics [writes Sulpicius], if their zeal to make more of a conquest than was necessary had not drawn them into the fray. Besides, if you ask my opinion, the accused and the accusers are equally unsavory. As for Ithacus, especially, I declare that he had no scruples, no respect for anything whatsoever. He is an arrogant, garrulous, impudent man, a spendthrift who refers everything to his belly and his gullet. He had gone so far in his foolishness to accuse all decent men, even saintly men who had a taste for reading or a firm purpose, of vying with one another in their fasting; he denounced them as accomplices or disciples of Priscillian.

And, what was even more serious in Sulpicius' view, this same Ithacus

> even dared at that time, the wretch, to attack Bishop Martin, a man who is in all respects equal to the apostles: he dared to reproach him publicly of belonging to that infamous heresy. Indeed, Martin was in Trèves at the time, and he unceasingly reprimanded Ithacus, exhorting him to drop the accusation. He begged Maximus not to shed the blood of the miserable men who were accused. It was quite enough, he said, that the guilty had been declared heretics by a tribunal of bishops and driven from their sees; it would be an unheard-of and monstrous novelty to have an ecclesiastical case judged by a secular magistrate.

We should note in passing that this was the opposite position to the one taken in 1229 by those who instituted the tribunals of the Inquisition. Martin's gesture and his intervention with the emperor were protests against something that would, indeed, be a perennial temptation in one part of the religious world, and that many of the saints managed to avoid: in the thirteenth century, Saint Ferdinand III of Spain would not admit the Inquisition in his kingdom; his cousin, the king of France, Louis IX, allowed the tribunals of the Inquisition to function, but refused the requests of the bishops to have the sentences of their councils carried out by secular judges.

What happened next in our story poisoned everything: Martin, who had to leave Trier, obtained from Emperor Maximus an assurance that no condemnation would be declared against the accused. But after he left, Maximus, outwitted by two bishops whose names Sulpicius mentions (Magnus and Rufus), put his prefect, Evodius, in charge of the case—a man whom Sulpicius describes as "pitiless and severe". Priscillian, convicted of sorcery and of immoral doctrines, admitted to having presided at "gatherings of fallen women", and ultimately, at the insistence of Evodius, the emperor sentenced Priscillian and his followers to the death penalty.

Later on, Martin was planning to return to Trier, where Emperor Maximus was protecting Bishop Ithacus with his imperial authority. Sulpicius says that he "met there the full force of the storm". Several bishops, even at Trier, were making common cause with Ithacus. At the arrival of Martin, "their hearts sank and there were many mutterings and quakings." The preceding day, the emperor had decided to send tribunes to Spain, armed with full authority, in order to track down the heretics and to deprive them of their properties and of life itself. "The bishops were well aware that all this would be exceedingly displeasing to Martin." They were especially afraid that Martin might refuse to be in communion with them. "They therefore came to an arrangement

. . . whereby palace officials should be sent to meet Martin and forbid him to come near the city unless he made a declaration that when he arrived he would be at peace with the bishops who were staying there" at Trier. Martin replied that "when he came he would be at peace with Christ". Having entered the city by night, he went to the church to pray, and then he showed up the next day at the palace. The emperor eluded his presence for two days. Sulpicius gives us to understand that Emperor Maximus coveted the goods of the men who were about to be condemned to death in order to fill the coffers of the state, which were always empty. And he makes an excuse for Maximus, who, he says, lived in almost constant fear of or in the midst of civil wars—the same sort of wars that had put him on the imperial throne in the first place.

The bishops who supported Ithacus used these two days to besiege Maximus. They said, "He [Martin] was no longer simply a protector of the heretics, but their avenger." "Indeed," Sulpicius Severus writes, "Maximus came very near to being persuaded to condemn Martin to share the fate of the heretics." Now, despite the carping of the bishops, Maximus knew very well where Martin stood and that, "in faith and holiness and spiritual power, [he] surpassed any man alive." Maxiumus therefore summoned Martin to the palace and insisted on conversing with him one-to-one. Maximus said that the heretics had been condemned through regular proceedings in the civil courts, and that only one bishop, Theognitus, had separated himself from his confreres and refused thereafter to be in communion with them, but that this was a case of personal animosity, not a condemnation of the action that they had taken against the Priscillianists. Martin would not be convinced. The emperor, in exasperation, abruptly left the room and gave the order to send to Spain those who had instructions to travel there to exterminate the followers of Priscillian.

When Martin learned that the order had been given, he returned to the palace. Night had fallen, but Martin managed to get a hearing. He promised that he would agree to be in communion with the bishops, provided that the tribunes who had been sent to Spain were recalled. "Maximus granted all his requests without delay", Sulpicius writes.

On the very next day a bishop named Felix was consecrated who was a stranger to the matters just described and quite worthy of the episcopal office. "On the same day Martin joined the bishops in communion, judging that to make this momentary concession was better than deserting the cause of those whose heads were in jeopardy. But though the bishops strove with all their might to get him to certify this communion with his signature, nothing would induce him to do that."

The next day Martin left Trèves (Trier). He was very unhappy, blaming himself for having given in to extortion. He was desolate over the fact that he had agreed to be in communion with the bishops who had arranged the condemnation of Priscillian. At the entrance to a town he let his companions go on ahead, sat down, and "went over and over in his mind the steps that had led up to this anguish of mind and the action he had taken". At that moment an angel came and admonished him: "'Martin,' said he, 'you have reason to feel compunction, but you had no other way out of your predicament. Rebuild your courage, get back your equanimity; or you will soon be imperilling not only your renown but your salvation.'" Martin set out again, with peace of mind, but from that moment on, during the remaining thirteen years[2] of

---

[2] Hoare's English translation has "thirteen"; the French text has *seize* (16), which could be a misreading of the handwritten word *treize* (13).—TRANS.

his life, he refused to go to synods and steered clear of all gatherings of bishops.

With the hindsight of history, it is obvious to us that Martin's attitude was quite sound: he opposed the intrusion of the civil authorities into spiritual matters and especially condemned the verdicts that were rendered against the heretics so as to sentence them to death or to any other temporal punishment. In his opinion, anathematizing and excommunicating a heretic when he refuses to submit to the Church's ruling is entirely legitimate, but he did not allow condemnations in the spiritual order to be combined with any temporal punishment.

The Priscillian affair weighed heavily upon him, and rightly so, since it has served over the centuries as an example—we will say it again—of a constant temptation that the Church has not always resisted. It should be noted also that when she succumbed and instituted the Inquisition, this expedient very soon turned against her. About sixty years later, under the reign of Philip the Fair, the French king declared that he was in charge of the fight against the heretics. Later on, it was a court of the Inquisition, made up of Parisian university professors, that would send Joan of Arc to be burned at the stake—to say nothing of the victims of that same institution, in Spain and elsewhere, at the end of the fifteenth century and throughout the sixteenth and seventeenth centuries. It appears to us significant that during that same era the shrine of Saint Martin, which had been the site of so many pilgrimages in the previous centuries, was gradually deserted; his tomb was destroyed, and his relics were scattered. Even if it was an entirely inadvertent development, perhaps it was more than just a coincidence.

9

The "Golden Legend" of Saint Martin

The works and deeds of Saint Martin constituted a sort of "golden legend" even before tradition had a chance to embroider upon them. We will mention one of the most amusing stories, the one about the Easter fish. On Easter day, indeed, Martin and his companions used to end their Lenten fast and eat fish. Now it happened that on one Easter day there was no fish in the monastery. The deacon Cato, the steward of the monastery and a skilled fisherman, said that he had tried all day but had caught nothing; even the other fisherman, who usually would sell their fish, had had no luck. "Go and let down your line," said Martin, "and a catch will follow." This happened at Marmoutier, where the lodgings of the monks are not far from the river. Sulpicius continues the story: "As we were having holidays for the Feast, we all set off to see the deacon fishing, everybody eagerly hoping that his attempts by Martin's orders to catch a fish for Martin's use would not be in vain."

Then, at the first cast of the line—a very small line, at that—the deacon pulled from the water an enormous pike fish, or maybe it wasn't a pike, but a salmon. In any case they made a real Easter feast of that miraculous catch.

On another occasion, in the same river, a snake was plowing the water and was headed for the bank where the monks stood. Martin said to it: "In the name of the Lord, I order you to go back." As Sulpicius tells it: "Immediately, at the saint's words, the noxious creature turned round and, as we watched it, swam across to the opposite bank. We could all see that there was something miraculous in this, but Martin sighed deeply. 'Snakes', he said, 'listen to me, and men refuse to listen.'"

Several miraculous events involving animals are related with regard to Martin, such as this story of the mad cow. Today we know about this sickness that sometimes seizes cows and drives them mad. One day, as Martin was returning from Trier, he heard loud bellowing and was alerted that a mad cow was coming. "She had left her herd and was attacking human beings and had gored several people dangerously." When she approached the group of monks who were traveling with the bishop, Martin raised his hand toward her and ordered her to stop.

> She drew up at his words and then stood motionless. At the same time Martin saw a demon perched on her back and spoke sternly to it. "Get off that animal, you pernicious creature," said he, "and stop tormenting an innocent beast." The wicked spirit obeyed and disappeared. The heifer had enough sense to know that she was liberated and, quite quiet now, she lay down at the saint's feet. Then he ordered her to go back to her herd and she rejoined her companions, as placidly as any sheep.

Another time, while making a tour of his parishes, Martin and his companions met a band of hunters.

> Their dogs were chasing a hare and the little thing was by this time exhausted by a long run, and there were open fields on all sides and no escape anywhere. More than once it had been on the point of being caught and it was only by frequent doublings that it was putting off immediate death. The man of blessings in his kindliness took compassion on it in its

danger and ordered the dogs to leave off following it and let the fugitive get away. They pulled up at once, at the first words of the order. You might have thought them chained or, rather, stuck fast in their own tracks. And so, with its pursuers pinned down, the little hare got safely away.

To remain for a moment in the animal kingdom, we should also report what Martin said when he spied "a sheep that had just been shorn": "It has fulfilled the Gospel precept", he observed. "It had two coats and has given one of them to someone who has none. You ought to do the same."

An even simpler story was told by Gallus while conversing with Sulpicius and their friend Postumianus; no doubt it can be attributed to that friend, for Gallus said that he would not mention the name of the person who witnessed the marvel, since that person was present among them. "A dog was barking at us rather violently and he said to it, 'In the name of Martin I order you to be silent.' And the dog was silent. The barking seemed to stick in his throat; you might have thought its tongue had been cut off. Yes, indeed," Gallus concluded, "the fact that Martin himself worked miracles is a small matter; believe me, many things were done by others using his name."

Gallus goes on to say a little further on:

It was only lately that I heard someone testifying how he had been sailing in the Tyrrhenian Sea, heading for Rome, when such a hurricane sprang up that all on board were in the utmost danger of their lives. In the middle of it all a certain Egyptian merchant who was not then a Christian shouted out: "God of Martin, save us." At once the storm was stilled, the sea died down and they held on their course in a great calm.

Yet things happened that were even more surprising than these somewhat ordinary miracles. Martin's friends insisted that he was occasionally visited by supernatural beings.

Gallus, when he relates the incident, calls Sulpicius as his witness. The two of them testify to the same fact:

> One day I and Sulpicius there were keeping watch outside Martin's door. We had already been sitting in silence for several hours, in deep awe and trepidation, as though we had been keeping our allotted watch before an angel's dwelling, though in fact, with the door of his cell closed, he did not know that we were there. We now heard the murmur of conversation and presently there came over us a kind of awe and stupefaction and we could not help being conscious of the presence of the divine.
>
> About two hours later Martin came out to us and then Sulpicius there, who could always speak to him more easily than anyone else, tried to persuade him to satisfy our pious thirst for knowledge by explaining the meaning of that holy awe which we agreed that we had both felt and telling us who had been in the conversation with him in his cell; for what we had heard outside the door had been a low and practically unintelligible murmur of voices.
>
> It was a long time before he would tell us, but there was nothing that Sulpicius could not drag out of him, however much against his will. At last he said—and I am going to tell you something scarcely believable, but as Christ is my witness I am not lying and no one would be so blasphemous as to suppose that Martin was lying—he said:
>
> "I will tell you, but please tell no one else. Agnes, Thecla and Mary were with me."
>
> He proceeded to describe to us the face and general appearance of each of them. He acknowledged also that he had had visits from them, not only that day but frequently. And he had to admit that he had quite often seen the Apostles Peter and Paul.

Indeed, the *Dialogues* of Sulpicius Severus, which are a supplement to the *Life* of Martin, begin by presenting the extraordinary deeds and exploits of the anchorites in the desert, so as to demonstrate later on that Martin is no less meritorious than those men who fled human society in order to consecrate themselves to God. One of the interesting things about this literary work is that it recalls for us all sorts of stories that were making the rounds then about the life of the Eastern hermits—stories that aroused so much interest in Martin in his youth that he wanted to imitate them.

So it is that Sulpicius' friend Postumianus tells him and their mutual friend Gallus the Gaul about his encounter with the hermit of Cyrene. Postumianus had boarded a boat at Narbonne and, after a stopover in Carthage, where he visited the tomb of Saint Cyprian, he set sail for Alexandria. A storm, however, forced him to land in a remote part of Cyrenaica. The region is a desert that lies between Egypt and the rest of northern Africa, a vast expanse of sand, where the shipwrecked men spied a sort of cabin made out of planks. They walked toward it and found there an old man turning a hand mill. After exchanging greetings, they explained to the old man that, since they had landed because of the storm, they wanted to see whether they could find any Christians in this desert. Postumianus tells how their host "burst into tears of joy and threw himself down at our knees".

> Kissing us again and yet again, he asked us to pray with him. Then he spread sheep-skins on the ground and made us sit down. He set before us a truly sumptuous lunch—half a loaf of barley bread! There were four of us, so with him there were five. He also brought a bunch of some herb whose name has slipped my memory. It was like mint, with an abundance of leaves, and tasted of honey. We found its exceedingly sweet taste delicious and had as much as we wanted of it.

At that, Sulpicius turns to Gallus and asks, "Well, what do you say about that lunch?" Gallus blushes slightly and exclaims,

That's just your way, Sulpicius, never to let an opportunity go by of teasing us about our appetites. But it's most inhumane of you to try and force us Gauls to live in angels' fashion, though I suspect that even angels take pleasure in eating! And as for that half loaf of barley bread, I should be afraid to start on it, even if I had it to myself. . . . [At most, it would do for the members of that party], whom I strongly suspect of having been put off their food by a good tossing at sea. But we are a long way from the sea here and, as I have frequently pointed out to you, we are Gauls.

Postumianus resumes his narrative, explaining that henceforth he will take care not to praise the moderation of anyone at all, so as not to upset the Gauls by presenting to them an example that would be too difficult to follow! That speaks volumes about the reputation of our [French] ancestors, for whom eating well was always very important.

As it turned out, the shipwrecked men stayed for a few days with that Cyrenian, who in reality was a priest. He brought them into a church made of plaited branches, where they assembled together with the other Christians of that locality. When they took leave, Postumianus offered him several gold pieces, which the priest indignantly refused to take: "Gold could break a Church sooner than build it." He accepted only a few garments, and the travelers bid him farewell so as to continue their journey toward Alexandria.

After that, Postumianus headed for the Upper Thebaid, that is, for the hinterlands of Egypt, where monks were numerous. They submitted to strict obedience to the authority of an abbot; some of them, with the permission of that abbot, lived a solitary life, and there are countless examples of hermits who worked miracles. One asked his abbot to stop sending him bread, and when the abbot went to see him, he saw hanging from the roof of the hut in which the hermit lived a basket made of palm leaves and filled with warm bread that appeared to be fresh from the oven. Another solitary lived on dates produced by a palm tree, which he would share with a lion that came to see him from time to time. Another was visited one day by a she-wolf that, in his absence, ate all by herself a loaf of bread, whereas he usually gave her the remaining fragments. After that she did not dare show herself and only returned seven days later, very meekly, with downcast eyes, as though utterly ashamed. The hermit gave her her portion of bread, and the she-wolf seemed to take courage, understanding that her mistake had been forgiven. Another holy man had become somewhat ill by eating poisonous plants; a gazelle approached him, so he threw to it the bunch of herbs that he had picked the previous day; the gazelle sorted out the poisonous plants and seemed to show the hermit which ones were safe to eat.

Postumianus noticed that, in places where the monks lived in community, their spirit of obedience obtained for them as many graces as were received by those who lived in solitude.

After enumerating all these examples, Sulpicius draws from the account what appears to him to be the obvious conclusion: "You certainly told us some very remarkable things but—if I may say so without offence to these holy men—there was absolutely nothing that I heard from you in which Martin was not their equal." He goes on to develop this idea:

> For when [the anchorites] perform those undoubtedly marvellous feats we hear of, they are free from all entanglements and have only heaven and the angels looking on. Martin, on the other hand, moved among crowds and in the haunts of men, amidst quarrelling clergy and raging bishops, and harassed by almost daily scandals on every side. Nevertheless, he stood unmoved amid all these things upon a foundation of unshakeable spiritual power and worked wonders unequalled

even by those dwellers in the desert, of our own or other days, of whom we have been hearing.

And he explains his reasoning: "Though you told us some remarkable things, you said nothing of anyone raising a dead man to life. That fact alone compels one to admit that no one can be compared with Martin."

There we have a posthumous eulogy of the bishop of Tours which manages to characterize very well what his sanctity accomplished: above and beyond the miracles, his sanctity consisted of his faith. Certified in his day by astounding miracles, this faith is apparent to us in his whole life. Although he was criticized by some contemporaries—notably by those who were elevated as he was to the episcopate but paid more attention to their own importance than to the Word that they were responsible for handing on—the people made no mistake about him. The external appearance of the man whom they had selected meant little to them; the people sensed and understood who Martin was, and would have expressed their view of him as Postumianus does: "So long as I live and think at all, I shall speak with admiration of the monks of Egypt, sing the praises of the anchorites, marvel at the hermits; but I shall always put Martin in a class by himself." The reason being that he was above all a man of faith and of prayer.

These reflections are invaluable for us today, first of all, because they put us back in an environment where there was opposition as well as praise. It is significant that some of the bishops who were Martin's confreres preferred to deny his virtues rather than to acknowledge their own shortcomings. Conversely, it is wonderful to see evidence of the devotion that the common people had for him—that *vox populi* without which no holy person can be recognized as a saint, in our time just as in his.

On the other hand, this sort of discussion characterizes very well Martin's holiness. He himself had dreamed of living as a hermit or an anchorite; he could not be either of those things; he might have eaten his heart out with regrets, imagining that he had missed his vocation! But in fact, forced to do something that he did not want to do, he accomplished much more than he could have dared to hope. He found a place for the absolute in everyday things. He gave up conversing with the lions, the she-wolves, or the gazelles of the wilderness, and went instead, on foot or riding his donkey, to be with the masses of peasants, scattered over the countryside, whom the gospel had not yet reached. By doing that, he converted, not a town, but a nation. He was a presence, a prayer in the midst of peasants who were given over to animism and superstitions. He did not often make use of his influence with the emperor, and, besides, when he did try he was only partially successful. His success was as humble as he was: little deeds done for little people—but it is thanks to him that steeples began to spring up in France, to the point where each village was able to have its own. To put it another way: he opened up a wide field for the gospel through the humble tone of his preaching, by going out to seek in their own homes those Gauls who loved the good life, and by making them into Christians.

In the following century Saint Patrick would likewise convert the Celts of Ireland—a land untouched by invasion or the Roman religion, where the people had not had to suffer persecution. The Celts of Ireland, like those in Gaul, would easily accept preaching about a God of Love and the fact that such a simple thing as a three-leafed clover should be a symbol for God the Father, the Son, and the Holy Spirit. For them, too, the absolute could be found in everyday things! Martin's approach, in its simplicity, would unleash their enthusiasm; all they needed to do was to accept the truth that they received everything from God. This is the faith that does not seek to work out reasons; the important thing is to contemplate the mystery and to trust that the mystery is a shining light. In such cases, very simple preaching that is accessible to everyone is also the only sort that will do. The faith is not an ideology; it can be explained without using words that end in "-ism". Faith presupposes a kind of adherence that is willing to receive rather than to discuss at first or to decide on one's own what to accept or not. Martin's faith was above all contemplation. It was a glance that illuminated at first and explained afterward. There was only one prerequisite: overturning the idols, whether it be coarse idols, like a statue of Jupiter or Venus, or a more subtle idol, like the sap that runs through the pine tree, enlivening it and pushing it to new heights, or like the spring that gushes from under a stone. Not to mention the idols with which the modern world swarms, which make an end out of what is merely a means, like money (which recalls the golden calf of the Bible) or the automobile, which is so practical but which it is so tempting to use in order to gratify one's passions or wild fantasies, so that it becomes a killing machine. Martin's faith, in its simplicity, became in itself a source of life capable of triumphing even over death.

10

The Death of Martin

Sulpicius Severus tells how he had fallen asleep one day in his cell.

> I suddenly seemed to see our holy Bishop Martin, dressed in a white robe, his face ablaze, his eyes like stars, his hair glowing red. He appeared to me in the same bodily form and features that I knew so well, but in such a way that—a thing not too easy for me to put into words—he could be recognized by them without its being possible actually to look at them.
>
> Smiling a little, he held out to me the book I had written on his life. I embraced his sacred knees and begged his blessing, as my custom was; and I felt the caressing touch of his hand upon my head as, among the formal words of the blessing, he repeated the Name of the Crucified, so familiar on his lips. But presently, while my eyes were still fixed upon him (for I could not have enough of the sight of his countenance) he was suddenly taken from me, snatched up on high. He traversed the immense spaces of the upper air and I was able, gazing intently, to follow him as he was swiftly borne upwards on a cloud; but, when the heavens had opened and received him, he could no longer be seen. Soon afterwards I saw the holy priest Clarus, who had lately died, ascend in the same way as his master.

I had the impertinence to want to follow him but, while I toiled and struggled to take the steep steps heavenwards, I woke up.

I shook off my sleep and had just begun to congratulate myself on the vision, when a boy of the household entered, looking unusually sad, and speaking and sobbing in the same breath. "What are you trying to tell me with such a sad face?" said I. "Two monks", he replied, "have just arrived from Tours. They have brought news that my lord Martin is dead."

Martin was around eighty years old and felt that his powers were diminishing, but all of a sudden he received a call: he was asked to come to the town of Candes, where violent disagreements had divided the clergy. Candes is located not far from Fontevraud, quite close to the place where the River Vienne flows into the Loire, about fifty kilometers from Tours. This was a request that he could not refuse; he made his way, therefore, to Candes, probably by riverboat, and soon he had reestablished peace among the quarreling clerics. One last anecdote that has the river as a backdrop:

He noticed on the river some water-fowl diving for fish and gorging their voracious crops with continual captures. "There", he said, "you have a picture of the demons. They lie in wait for the unwary, catch them before they know, devour them when they have caught them, and are never satisfied with those they have devoured." Then, exercising over those birds the same authority with which he used to put the demons to flight, he ordered them with words of power to leave the stream in which they were swimming and betake themselves to waterless and unfrequented regions. At this, all the wild-fowl formed themselves into a flock and, flying in one body, left the river and made for the mountains and forests. There were many witnesses and it caused them no little astonishment to see in Martin powers so great that he could even order birds about.

Again and again we have related anecdotes of this sort. In Martin's story there are pages from a "golden legend" highlighting his kinship with the anchorites living in the wilderness, where it seems to them quite natural that a lioness should come looking for them to make them understand that they had to go and take care of her cubs, or that a she-wolf should ask pardon for having devoured their ration of bread in their absence. And then there are similar scenes of Martin himself giving orders to dogs who are chasing a hare. Here, he drives away the water-fowl whose voraciousness seems to him excessive, and he makes them into symbols of the demons.

In any case, after spending some time at Candes, now that peace had been restored, Martin felt that he was losing his strength.

> He called the brethren together and informed them that the end had come. Then indeed did sorrow and grief fall upon all. This prompted him to pray to the Lord. Distressed by their wailing, and lying on the ground upon a bed of ashes, he prayed: "Lord, this warfare in the body is a heavy burden and to have fought until now is enough. But if it is Thine order that I toil on still, maintain guard over the camp of Thy people, I do not refuse, nor plead the feebleness of age. I will consecrate myself to the fulfilment of the duties Thou dost lay upon me; I will fight on under Thy banners, so long as it is Thy command. Sweet to an old man is release after labour, but the will can triumph over length of life and knows no yielding to old age. But shouldst Thou now be indulgent to my years, it is Thy will, O Lord, and it is good. As for these for whom I fear, Thou Thyself wilt be their guardian.

Martin never chose his own lot, no more so in the face of death than in life; he was not the one to decide. His disciples urged him to allow them to offer him some relief and tried to wrap him in a blanket, or at the very least to help him to turn over. Martin ordered them, "Let me keep my eyes on heaven rather than on earth." At that, the devil stood beside him once again. Martin addressed him: "Why are you standing there, blood-thirsty beast? You will find nothing for yourself in me, you dismal creature. Abraham's bosom is awaiting me."

"With these words, he yielded up his spirit."

And Sulpicius Severus adds that those who looked upon his face at that moment saw that it was like the face of an angel, that his limbs seemed as white as snow, so that those who were present said, " 'Who would have thought that he had been covered with sackcloth and lain in ashes?' For he already looked as he will appear with transfigured body in the glory of the resurrection to come."

Sulpicius continues with a beautiful description of Martin's funeral, which he compares to a "triumph", the triumphant procession of a Roman general through the cheering crowds. But first let us turn to the detailed account that Gregory of Tours[1] gives of how the body of Martin was carried off.

Martin, he says, died in the middle of the night on Sunday (November 8, 397); at his death many people heard a concert in the heavens.

As soon as the man of God fell ill, the inhabitants of Poitiers joined the people of Tours in keeping vigil and awaiting his departure. When he died, a lively dispute arose between the two groups.

> The men of Poitiers said: "As a monk he is ours. He became an abbot in our town. We entrusted him to you, but we demand him back. It is sufficient for you that, while he was a

---

[1] The citations are taken from Gregory of Tours, *The History of the Franks*, trans. and with an introduction by Lewis Thorpe (London: Penguin Books, 1974), pp. 98–99. After the words "November 11", the citations are again from Sulpicius Severus.—TRANS.

Bishop on this earth, you enjoyed his company, you shared his table, you were strengthened by his blessing and above all you were cheered by his miracles. Let all these things suffice for you, and permit us at least to carry away his dead body."

And so, when news arrived of Martin's illness, the people of Poitiers had hastened to Candes, where he was staying, and now they claimed the right to bury him in their city. But they ran up against serious opposition.

To this the men of Tours replied: "If you say that we should be satisfied with the miracles which he performed for us, then admit that while he was with you he did more than in our town. If all his other miracles are left out of the count, he raised two dead men for you and only one for us; and, as he himself used often to say, his miraculous power was greater before he was made Bishop than it was afterwards. It was therefore necessary that what he did not achieve with us when he was alive he should complete now that he is dead. God took him away from you, but only so that He might give him to us. If the custom established by the men of old is observed, then by God's will he shall be buried in the town where he was consecrated. If you propose to claim him because you have his monastery, then you must know this, that his first monastery was in Milan."

The quarrel was typical of that era: a time when people began to attach enormous importance to relics, a trend that would continue unabated. Martin died at Candes and ended up being claimed simultaneously by the people of his diocese in Tours and by those in Poitiers who were acquainted with him at the time when he was appointed bishop.

But let us listen to the outcome of the story:

They went on with their argument until the sun went down and night began to fall. The body was placed in the middle of the room, the doors were locked and he was watched over by the two groups. The men of Poitiers planned to carry off the body as soon as morning came, but Almighty God would not allow the town of Tours to be deprived of its patron. In the end all the men of Poitiers fell asleep in the middle of the night, and there was not one who remained on guard. When the men of Tours saw that all the Poitevins had fallen asleep, they took the mortal clay of that most holy body and some passed it out through the window while others stood outside to receive it. They placed it on a boat and all those present rowed down the River Vienne. As soon as they reached the River Loire, they set their course for the city of Tours, praising God and chanting psalms. The men of Poitiers were awakened by their voices and they went back home in great confusion, taking nothing of the treasure which they were supposed to be guarding.

What is certain is that Martin died on November 8 and that his funeral was solemnly celebrated in Tours on November 11. "No one could believe what a vast multitude gathered for the funeral. The whole city poured out to meet the body. Everyone from the farms and the villages was there, and many even from the surrounding towns. . . . It is said that nearly two thousand of them were assembled on that day." In a moving description, Sulpicius Severus mentions that among the two thousand present was "the consecrated virgin choir",

> abstaining from the unseemliness of weeping and concealing their grief under a holy joy. But though the strength of their faith might forbid them to weep, their feelings forced a sigh. . . . You could pardon their weeping; you could join in their rejoicing. For every man owed it to himself to weep, and to Martin to rejoice.
>
> Thus this multitude, chanting the hymns of heaven, accompanied the body of the man of blessings to the place of burial.

This is proof enough of the immense procession that accompanied Martin's funeral ceremonies, the crowd of his companions, among them the brethren from Marmoutier, but also the gathering of virgins—at a time when monasteries for women were still only a shadow of what they became later on. This was the age when the first of those monasteries was being established in Palestine under the aegis of Saint Jerome; and yet these Christian virgins were gathered here, witnessing to their hope with regard to Martin, which tempered their mourning. The whole retinue resounded also with the melody of "the hymns of heaven"; in those days the faithful departed individual was accompanied by the chanting of psalms. It was a funeral cortege in which the crowd combined its expression of mourning with the beauty of sacred song.

And in conclusion there is something that comes quite naturally from the pen of Sulpicius Severus: it is, as we have seen, the comparison between this funeral procession and a triumph, which in antiquity was a grand ceremony honoring the victorious military leaders. The allusion is not uncalled for with respect to Martin, since he was a soldier early in life; and in the right circumstances, had he continued in that career, it could have ended in a "triumph" of the same kind.

There could have been no better way, at the end of the fourth century, of emphasizing the turning point in civilization that had been reached. We sense that the author is acutely aware of his own times: the sort of awareness that generally is attained only after a number of years, when one is able to survey past events as a whole. His reflections at this juncture are quite outstanding:

> Compare it, if you like, with a worldly pageant— . . . a triumphal procession. What can you find in that to rival Martin's obsequies? Let others drive before their chariots

captives with hands bound behind their backs; Martin's body was followed by those who, with him for their leader, have overcome the world. Let others have the honour of the disordered clappings of a frenzied populace. Martin was applauded with sacred psalmody; Martin was honoured by celestial songs.

A powerful image for the changing of the guard occasioned by the new civilization, the one replacing cruel antiquity and opening up for all men new perspectives that were made possible by the faith! "Martin, the poor man, the lowly, goes rich into heaven." The burial of that exemplary Christian gave full expression to the hopes of Martin and of others like him who had chosen the way of the gospel. To a much greater extent than they supposed, they were changing an entire civilization, leaving the cruelty of dominion by the force of arms and entering the hard-won joy of ongoing victory over self, which has an unexpected consequence: a sort of universal exultation that triumphs over death even in the midst of a funeral ceremony. No doubt about it, nothing better exemplifies, at the end of the fourth century, the momentousness of the advance that had just been made by an entire civilization than the funeral procession of Martin.

11

Devotion to Saint Martin

The feast of Saint Martin, November 11, was a holy day of obligation, and hence a holiday from work, until the end of the Middle Ages. It was celebrated likewise on July 4 as the feast of "*Saint-Martin-le-Bouillant*", recalling the translation of Saint Martin's body to its eventual resting place. Later on other feasts would be instituted, celebrating on May 12 "The Subvention", that is, the assistance offered by Saint Martin when the Normans were defeated in the year 903; this became the occasion for masquerades and also for a procession of the religious community at Marmoutier to the tomb of Saint Martin of Tours. Finally, there was "The Reversion of Saint Martin", December 13, which commemorated the return of the saint's relics after the Norman invasions; this feast was instituted by the Council of Tours in 912. As you see, Saint Martin's place in the liturgical calendar was very well established from olden times. We should also mention the feast of the Translation of the Head of Saint Martin, instituted by Pope John XXII in 1323. It was celebrated on December 1. Note also that, for a long time, the liturgical year used to begin on November 11; that was the first day of Advent, the penitential time of preparation for the Feast of Christmas.

In Tours, the place where Saint Martin's cape, or *capella*, was preserved, became so popular that it gave rise to a term that is now commonly used in French: *chapelle*, meaning "chapel".

This simple observation is enough to indicate the extraordinary diffusion of anything having to do with Saint Martin. For starters, consider his name in the French-speaking population. Glance at any yearbook, and you will find twice as many Martins as Duponts or Durands, not to mention those with the surnames Martineau, Martinez, Dammartin, etc. It is by far the most common name among the French, and the same goes for place names; it is said that some pages in the listing of the townships in France read like a litany of the saints. Now, of these townships, more than four hundred, located in all the provinces, bear the name of Saint Martin: Saint-Martin-Belle-Roche in the Saône area, Saint-Martin-de-Boscherville in Normandy, Saint-Martin-de-Londres in the region of Hérault, Saint-Martin-de-Crau in Provence, Saint-Martin-du-Var in the south of France, Saint-Martin-du-Bois in Anjou, Saint-Martin-des-Champs in Brittany, and Saint-Martin-les-Langres or Saint-Martin-l'Heureux in the east. As the patron of meadows, woods, or rivers, he is everywhere. And what can we say about the number of churches dedicated to him! In the nineteenth century, the historian Lecoy de la Marche counted 3,678 parishes in France alone; if you go over to the British Isles, you find 163 parishes, six of which are in the city of London alone; the count is 75 in Holland, 239 in Flanders, more than 100 in Hungary, 120 in [the former] Yugoslavia, and even more in Spain, Italy, and Germany.[1]

---

[1] On this subject we cite the excellent article concerning the *"Rayonnement du culte de saint Martin en France et dans le monde"* ["The spread of devotion to

"Wherever Christ is known, Martin is honored", Venantius Fortunatus exclaimed as early as the sixth century. In his day, the pilgrimage to Saint Martin of Tours was the most important one in France. Fortunatus himself traveled to the basilica that had been dedicated on July 4, 470, to the memory of Saint Martin and contained his tomb. One of Martin's successors in the episcopal see, Gregory of Tours, did much in that same century to make the tomb of Saint Martin of Tours "the greatest pilgrimage place in Gaul".[2]

At that time the custom of *laus perennis*, of perpetual praise, was established in Tours, at the tomb of Saint Martin. Day and night clerics took turns chanting psalms there, and this practice would be kept up for a long time through the efforts of other monasteries: in the time of Abelard, for example, the custom was still being continued at the monastery of Saint-Marcel de Chalon, where teams of monks relayed day and night, so that the praise was never interrupted.

We should mention that this practice of perpetual praise was established by Saint Brice [Brictio], who succeeded Martin as bishop in the year 397. The same man who, as we have seen, had had several run-ins with his bishop founded a college of clerics in order to ensure that the praises of God would be sung perpetually around his tomb, day and night. It must also be noted that his episcopacy was no less turbulent: because of serious charges brought against him (he was accused of having had a child by a nun!), he had to go to Rome to defend himself, and he remained there for seven years. When he returned, he once again governed the episcopal see:

Saint Martin in France and throughout the world"], which appeared in 1959 in the periodical *Sanctuaires et pèlerinages* with the by-line of Canon J. Sadoux, then rector of Saint-Martin de Tours.

[2] To quote a phrase used by Brigitte Beaujard at the international congress held at Tours in 1994 concerning Saint Gregory of Tours.

he had been found innocent, and in his final years he distinguished himself by his irreproachable sanctity. His feast falls on November 13, two days after that of Saint Martin, from whom he had obviously learned patience. After Brice, Saint Perpetuus continued the custom of perpetual praise, which was destined to go on through the centuries and which noticeably influenced the liturgy of the Divine Office. The Council of Vannes in 465 prescribed that the office should be recited in the manner that had been inaugurated by the tomb of Saint Martin.

It is a question not only of the history of religious devotions, but of history plain and simple. Tours, with the tomb of Saint Martin, was to be an irreplaceable way station: we must not forget that Clovis [the king of the Franks] went there twice. Gregory of Tours relates his expeditions in his usual manner, always lively and full of marvelous details. Tours, site of the tomb of the holy bishop of whom he was the successor, was at the border between the territories conquered by the Franks and those that belonged then to the Goths. The latter, as we have seen, were Christians, but heretics—Arians, whose beliefs went back to the preaching of Ulfila. Gregory mentions at first an interview that is said to have taken place in Amboise, between Clovis and Alaric, the king of the Goths; they had promised each other friendship and left in peace. But if we are to believe Gregory, "At that time a great many people in Gaul were very keen on having the Franks as their rulers."

An account of the events follows: " 'I find it hard to go on seeing these Arians occupy a part of Gaul', said Clovis to his ministers. 'With God's help let us invade them. When we have beaten them, we will take over their territory.' They all agreed to this proposal. An army was assembled and Clovis marched on Poitiers."

The army of the Goths was near Poitiers at that time, and Gregory lingers over several anecdotes. As he was leading his troops through the region of Tours, Clovis, "in respect for Saint Martin, ordered that they should requisition nothing in this neighbourhood except fodder and water". At that, a soldier from the army seized some bales of hay in a field and took them from their owner, "a poor man", saying: "Well, this is fodder. We shan't be disobeying his orders if we take it." The incident was reported to Clovis, who immediately struck the soldier with his sword and exclaimed, "It is no good expecting to win this fight if we offend Saint Martin!" The chronicler adds, "This was enough to ensure that the army took nothing else from this region."

Clovis, meanwhile, dispatched several envoys to the tomb of the saint in Tours, laden with gifts, and prayed: "Lord God, if You are on my side and if You have decreed that this people of unbelievers, who have always been hostile to You, are to be delivered into my hands, deign to show me a propitious sign as these men enter Saint Martin's church, so that I may know that You will support your servant Clovis." Now the king's delegates, the moment that they entered the basilica, heard the cantor begin to intone the psalm: "For thou didst gird me with strength for the battle; thou didst make my assailants sink under me. Thou didst make my enemies turn their backs to me, and those who hated me I destroyed" [Ps 18:39–40 RSVC]. We need not add that they were delighted by this favorable omen; they presented their gifts and hastened back to announce to the king what they had heard.

Once the army had arrived on the banks of the River Vienne, it was not long before it experienced divine favor: the river had swollen as a result of heavy rains, yet a doe crossed over it, showing them the ford by which the soldiers could make the crossing. Clovis himself arrived in the vicinity of Poitiers, and he seemed to see from afar a pillar of fire rising from the basilica of Saint Hilary, like a beacon that indicated "the support of the blessed Saint". He repeated to the army the prohibition against pillaging any goods at all in those lands and along the way; then the clash with Alaric's armies took place in Vouillé. "The Goths fled, as they were prone to do", Gregory notes, adding that King Clovis was victorious by the grace of God. With the help of his son Thierry, Clovis was to subdue the entire region. He spent the winter at Bordeaux, carried off all the treasure that Alaric had amassed in Toulouse, and marched on Angoulême, which surrendered immediately. Soon he returned to Tours and "gave many gifts to the basilica of Saint Martin". It was there that he was clothed with the imperial insignia. "Letters reached Clovis from Emperor Anastasius to confer the consulate on him. In Saint Martin's church he stood clad in a purple tunic and the military mantle, and he crowned himself with a diadem." His authority thus received a sort of imperial approval—a curious vestige of the time when the Roman Empire was a reality.

Gregory adds: "He then rode out on his horse and with his own hand showered gold and silver coins among the people present all the way from the doorway of Saint Martin's church to Tours cathedral. From that day on he was called Consul or Augustus." The battle of Vouillé took place in the year 507, and Clovis would continue with another string of victories. It is well known that he died in Paris (November 27, 511) after attending the council that established the right of asylum in Gaulish territories. It is impossible to overstate the importance of this right of asylum, which would be enjoyed by all the churches that were multiplying on French soil at that time—even by the simple *calvaires* [shrines] at the crossroads—in the development of morality. When we recall the harshness of punishments under Roman law, we can appreciate the thoroughgoing progress brought about by this institution, which gave a second chance even to the worst criminals—progress that would only be consolidated and spread during the entire period that we call the "Middle Ages"; the right of asylum would not disappear until the sixteenth century, under the provisions of the bourgeois courts.[3]

But we could not leave the chronicle of Gregory of Tours without quoting what follows: "After the death of her husband Queen Clotilde came to live in Tours. She served as a religious in the church of Saint Martin. She lived all the rest of her days in this place, apart from an occasional visit to Paris. She was remarkable for her great modesty and her loving kindness."

The veneration of the tomb of Saint Martin in Tours was a phenomenon that presided over the inauguration of the authentic Christian faith in the kingdom, over that decisive choice made by Clovis under the influence of his wife, Clotilde, at a time when the Goths, the Vandals, and also the Burgundians who were battling on French soil were spreading the Arian heresy, which in Spain, for example, would not be obliterated until the mid-seventh century.

The thoroughgoing transformation that took place in the populace was rendered visible through the various modes of artistic expression, and this is probably the most significant

---

[3] The right of asylum existed in antiquity, but in a very restricted form: the only one who could benefit from it was a person who had made his way into the temple. The temples of Roman antiquity were now few and far between, unlike the churches in our French parishes and the shrines at the crossroads.

sign of a change in the general mentality. Indeed, it may be surprising to see that the churches that were springing up just about everywhere, and even the basilicas that were constructed at the behest of the emperors and with their financial support, resembled the pagan temples neither in their architecture—which had to take into account the crowds that would come and fill them, whereas previously temples were strictly for priests—nor in their external appearance: sculpture, especially monumental sculpture, had been the art of Greco-Roman antiquity par excellence. Now, as in the fourth century, we can observe that color assumes an importance in architecture that no one had dreamed of before. This was true even in the era of the catacombs: Isn't it surprising that these subterranean places of worship, in a time when lighting was scarce (just a few oil lamps or wax candles), display a profusion of color? Upon reflection we realize that there was an absolutely astounding contrast between the actual living conditions of those people who gathered to pray in hiding and the vitality expressed there through their art. The paintings in the catacombs, we must admit, are a real question mark in the history of art. In a place where one might have expected, if anything, the art of bas-relief, the art of the colorist is born, which is related to Alexandrine painting yet is distinctive in that it entirely covers the surfaces of the meeting rooms with a multiplicity of symbols, indicating that those spaces were considered not only from a practical perspective but also from an aesthetic point of view. A depiction of a meal stands for the Last Supper, and the herdsman carrying a lamb on his shoulders is the Good Shepherd. A pagan who made his way into these underground galleries would have seen nothing that could have shocked him; he probably would have made the same remark as a certain nineteenth-century art historian: that it was "a degenerate art used for poor people".

Now when those same poor people were erecting basilicas in the fourth century, with the support of the emperors, they did not take the opportunity to decorate them like the temples in that same century, with a profusion of statues. Color triumphed once again, this time in the splendid form of the mosaic. The Romans used to decorate their floors with mosaics against a white background; but here backgrounds of blue or gold would be more common, because they were inspired by the same quest for color. In the fifth century the Italian city of Ravenna witnessed the production of a whole series of these masterpieces, which people still visit and admire in our day, although for a long time they were looked down on by art history "connoisseurs". By the beginning of the fifth century the city had become an imperial capital; it would remain such for almost two centuries: even though after the empire came to an end in 476 it was only the capital of the Gothic kings, for instance, Odovacar or Theodoric, who succeeded the Romans. For us, Ravenna is the capital of that new art that began to develop in the fourth century and produced masterpieces such as the two processions of saints, one of men and one of women, at Saint-Apollinaire-le-Neuf. The magnificent mausoleum of Galla Placidia is a brilliant fifth-century example of this colorful art, which entirely covers the walls and the vaults and displays the story of Christ and various scenes from the Bible, emphasizing the architectural arrangement without disrupting it, and enlivening the entire structure.

For from then on this seems to have been the main preoccupation of the builders: to *enliven* the meeting place; hence the use of color, which is life itself. No longer was there any concern about the exact representation of reality; the purpose of this art was not to make reality present again but, rather, to transcend it. This was the origin of the icon, which, instead

of representing reality, reveals what classical portraiture concealed. The icon has in view only that interior being it strives
to reveal; measurements, perspective, the laws of anatomy
have little importance; it is designed to evoke a truth, and its
domain is the interior life. The icon makes the viewer see
what nature can disguise; it is a different look at man and at
life. Furthermore, it had a separate destiny. Born in those
distant times when classical civilization was tottering, along
with its characteristic means of expression, the icon perpetu-
ated and propagated itself especially in the Churches of the
East. Despite the militant resistance that it met with in the
Byzantine Empire, it took root and spread through the Or-
thodox Christian communities; later on it had a privileged
place in Russian art. In the West it experienced vicissitudes
of a different sort, but today its spiritual depths are being
rediscovered.

At any rate, far from leading to an impoverishment, this
new concept was to enrich artistic vision to an extraordinary
degree—all the more so because of a momentous event that
occurred in the life of Christianity during the fifth century:
the conversion of Ireland. It was in the year 432 that Saint
Patrick began an evangelization that would prove to be extremely swift and fruitful: like the Celts in Gaul, those of
Ireland (who did not have to endure Roman rule) would
joyfully accept faith in one God in Three Persons, a God of
love who is infinitely "other" and infinitely near, since he
became man. Less than a century would pass before these
same Irishmen would come to Europe to revive the faith,
which was threatened by a multitude of heresies, and they
would bring with them their concept of art, which we can
discern in Gaulish art, where it would be displayed with an
astonishing exuberance before giving birth later on to Romanesque art, strictly speaking. Even a historian such as

Henri Marrou, whose preference for classical art is not in question, was struck, in his study of late antiquity, by what he calls "the invasion of the *entrelacs* [interlacing figures]". Far from being a simple decorative motif, as in Greek art, for example, from the sixth century on these interlacing figures became a real artistic mainstay, which would render both animal subjects and, even more strikingly, the letters of the alphabet, breathing a mysterious life into their unpredictable meanderings, animating them with a sort of hidden and unexpected vitality that is ever new: a vitality still found in the illuminated initial letters of twelfth-century manuscripts. The art of the colorist, the art of internal movements that often reveal a baffling imagination—these are the elements of a form of artistic expression that is completely distinct from that of classical antiquity and that would be ensconced in the period we call the High Middle Ages, from which, unfortunately, few examples have come down to us, since most of them fell victim to the incomprehension and rage that followed the "medieval" period.

Now the tomb of Saint Martin is a striking example of what was to happen over the course of the centuries. Gregory of Tours has related how, after he became the nineteenth bishop of the city, he found that the cathedral,

> in which Saint Martin and all these other priests of the Lord had been consecrated to the episcopal office, had been destroyed by fire and was in a sorry state of ruin. I rebuilt it, [he informs us,] bigger and higher than before, and in the seventeenth year of my episcopate I re-dedicated it. . . . I found the walls of Saint Martin's church damaged by fire. I ordered my workmen to use all their skill to paint and decorate them, until they were as bright as they had previously been.

Recall that the first edifice had been consecrated by Saint Perpetuus in the year 470; it was, the chroniclers assure us, the greatest basilica that had been built in the West until the time of Charlemagne's empire: one hundred sixty feet long, sixty feet wide, and the vaulted ceiling forty-five feet high.

At the time of the Norman invasions in 903, the basilica was seriously endangered. While the Normans were attacking the ramparts, one part of the population of Tours had the idea of carrying the reliquary of Saint Martin in procession all the way up to the city walls; they then stood and prayed for his intercession at one of the gates that the attackers were threatening to break down. At that moment the Normans, suddenly seized with panic, left off their attack, and fled. Subsequently the basilica itself would be surrounded by bulwarks; they called it Martinopolis, the city of Martin. When Pope Urban II came to summon Christendom to undertake a crusade to liberate Jerusalem from the Muslims, he stopped at the tomb of Saint Martin. Someone else would also pay her respects there one day: Joan of Arc, who came to Tours in 1429 to have her armor fashioned.

The pilgrimage that led to the tomb of Saint Martin was called "the pilgrimage of Gaul" during the Council of Orleans in 511, which ranks it as the equivalent of the pilgrimage to Rome or to Jerusalem. This pilgrimage was of great importance, as documents over the centuries repeatedly attest. It was mentioned, for instance, at the Council of Chalon-sur-Saône in 813, where it was declared as important as a pilgrimage to Rome. In the following century, Pope Leo VII declared, in 938: "No place, with the exception of Saint Peter's in Rome, draws such a great number of suppliants, coming from such different and distant lands." This is confirmed by Odo, the abbot of Cluny, who speaks of "the earnestness of the foreigners, the constant stream of thousands of people whose very language is unknown"; these were the throngs that poured in through the doors of the basilica that was erected over the tomb. Yet this was the century in which the pilgrimage of Saint James of Compostela had become the third most important place of pilgrimage in Christendom, right after Rome and Jerusalem.

Now, in the *Pilgrim's Guide* for that same pilgrimage of Santiago de Compostela, there is a lengthy note about the tomb of Saint Martin: "One who travels this road should likewise pay a visit, on the banks of the Loire River, to the venerable remains of Saint Martin, bishop and confessor. That is the place where he died, the miracle-worker who gloriously brought three dead men back to life and restored lepers, the possessed, the infirm, the insane and demoniacs as well as other sick people to health." A description of the tomb itself of Saint Martin then follows:

> The reliquary where his precious remains rest, nearby the city of Tours, is resplendent with a profusion of gold, silver, and precious stones; it is renowned for working frequent miracles. Above it, an immense and venerable basilica has been erected in his honor, on a grand scale, modeled on the Church of Saint James. Sick people come here and are cured, the possessed are delivered, the blind see, the lame walk, and all sorts of illnesses are healed, and everyone who asks for graces receives consolation and strength. That is why the fame of its glory has spread everywhere in panegyrics that rightly honor Christ. The saint's feast day is celebrated on the eleventh of November.[4]

[4] Excerpt from the edition of the *Guide du pèlerin de Saint-Jacques de Compostelle* (Pilgrim's guide to Saint James of Compostela) compiled by Jeanne Vieillard (Mâcon, 1950). One paragraph in this work notes the close relationship that exists, even from the architectural point of view, between the church of Santiago de Compostela and the church of Saint Martin of Tours, which was rebuilt in the seventh century and has been preserved as almost the only monument to that exalted period of architecture.

The utter destruction of the tomb did not occur until the sixteenth century, when the Huguenots leveled it "to its foundations" in 1562, burned the relics, and scattered the ashes. The reliquary containing Martin's remains was consumed in a furnace, from which the dismayed church warden, Saugeron, who was present at the scene, was able to recover a part of the skull and a few bones. The basilica survived (this was the one dating from the twelfth century, begun in 1175 and completed at the beginning of the thirteenth century); the pilgrimages were soon back in business; but the ravages would begin all over again with the French Revolution. In 1793 the basilica was handed over to plunderers, while the building itself was used as a stable. For lack of maintenance, it deteriorated so much and so rapidly that in 1797 the vaults collapsed; after that it remained in ruins and suffered the degradations to which every monument of that sort is exposed, serving as a quarry for anyone who wanted to carry out a construction project at its expense. It was not until after the Reign of Terror was over that it was discovered that the relics of Saint Martin had been removed and concealed by a bell-ringer named Lhommais.

These are names to be remembered, names of very humble folk—the kind Martin of Tours loved—who braved danger and risked much in order to save from fire and slaughter whatever could be saved. It takes a lot of courage—a strong personality—to go against a mass movement, especially in an age like that of the French Revolution.

No doubt we should also remember, despite or perhaps precisely because of his simplicity, the name of Monsieur Dupont, "the holy man of Tours", who in the nineteenth century was dismayed to see that no one in his town knew any

more the location of Saint Martin's tomb. He purchased the
houses at the intersection of the rue Descartes and the rue des
Halles, which had been built on the spot where the ancient
basilica had stood, and began to excavate. Then on December
21, 1880 (the day after the feast of the Reversion of Saint
Martin), fragments of a tomb came to light: it was the one in
which Martin had been buried on July 4, 470. Therefore the
construction of a new basilica was begun, which slowly took
shape and was eventually dedicated on July 4, 1925. After
almost two centuries of neglect, it is possible once again in
our day to kneel and pray over the remains of Saint Martin.
Of course, the setting is no longer what it once had been; the
reconstruction bears the hallmarks of that helplessness in the
presence of beauty that characterized the nineteenth century,
from the religious perspective. But at last the holy place has
been rediscovered and honored.

What remains to be said on the subject of recollections about
Martin belongs more to folklore than to the veneration of the
saints: for instance, the festivals of Saint Martin to the north
of France in Belgium, in Ieper, Ghent, or Dunkirk, which
have maintained a popular character, and even in Holland, in
Groningen, for example.

His feast day is well situated on the calendar, since it occurs
at the time when the harvests have come in and the grape
gathering is over; a time when people like to congregate,
especially in the countryside; 'tis the season to eat Saint
Martin's goose and drink Saint Martin's wine, that period of
clearer, sunnier weather that cuts through the autumn mists
somewhat. It is possible that Thanksgiving Day in the United
States, although connected with the particular circumstances
of the European emigration, may have been influenced by

the memory of the popular merrymaking that took place in autumn around the feast of Saint Martin.[5]

We should emphasize also the importance over the centuries of the work by Sulpicius Severus narrating the *Life of Martin of Tours*, a book that ever since the fourth century has been what we would call a best-seller. Sulpicius himself, in his *Dialogues*, recorded his conversation with one of his friends, Postumianus, who had come to see him in his retreat in Alzonne; he hastens to tell Sulpicius: " 'Your book is never out of reach of my hand. Look, here it is! Do you recognize it?' And he displayed the book which had been concealed in his dress. 'It has been my companion by land and sea. In all my travels it has been my friend and comforter.' " And he goes on to enumerate all the countries where he has determined that people were reading the *Life of Martin of Tours*, by Sulpicius Severus.

> There is practically no place in the world where the contents of this delightful story have not become public property. The first man to bring it to Rome was your great admirer Paulinus [of Nola]. Then the whole city began fighting for it and I saw the booksellers in raptures. They looked upon it as a record profit-maker because nothing sold more quickly or fetched a better price.
>
> The book travelled well ahead of me and by the time I got to Africa it was being read all over Carthage. The only man who had not got it was that priest in Cyrenaica, and *he* made a copy of it when I lent it to him. And as for Alexandria, nearly everybody there knows it better than you do! It has travelled all over Egypt, Nitria, the Thebaid and all the Memphite realms. I saw it being read by an old man in the

[5] These different sorts of festivities have been described in the previously cited article by Canon Sadoux, rector of Saint Martin of Tours, in the periodical *Sanctuaires et pèlerinages* (1959). They were also the subject of a special issue of the periodical *Fêtes et Saisons*, no. 53 (Paris: Éditions du Cerf, 1950).

desert, and, when I told him that I was a friend of yours, he
and a number of other brethren commissioned me, if ever I
got back to this country and found you safe and sound, to
make you fill in the gaps which you said in your book you
had left, with the blessed man's other miracles.

It is quite difficult for us to imagine such a widespread
diffusion of a work in an age when each book had to be
copied out by hand. Yet a witness attests to the fact. A witness
who is not afraid to give his name and who displays as much
interest as the readers of whom he speaks. The work appeared in 397, the same year as the death of Martin, and the
readers of it were still asking Sulpicius Severus for further
details about Martin's life and miracles.

The work deserves it, since it was written by a contemporary who was conscientious, albeit enthusiastic, who affec-
tionately describes everything that he could learn about Saint
Martin and who knows how to communicate his ardor; then,
too, very early on his work was utilized and adapted by other
authors. In the fifth century it was versified by Paulinus of
Périgueux, a friend of Bishop Perpetuus, bishop of Tours
from 461 to 491, the same one who erected and dedicated the
first basilica in honor of Saint Martin; the biography was later
adapted more felicitously by Venantius Fortunatus, a great
poet who lived in the latter half of the sixth century. A
number of medieval authors described his life, beginning
with Gregory of Tours, who also coined a happy expression:
"Martin, the special patron of the whole world" (*Toto orbi
peculiari patrono*). In the nineteenth century Lecoy de la
Marche, in his exhaustive study, enumerated the principal
literary works devoted to Saint Martin: works written by
Richer, abbot of Saint-Martin-de-Nesse, in the twelfth century; by Walafrid Strabon or Notker, abbot of Saint-Gall, in
the ninth century. People also used to tell the tale (which

became a *fabliau*, or medieval short story) of the two sick men who heard that the relics of Saint Martin were being carried in procession and therefore fled from one street to the next, convinced that if the relics passed by they would be cured, which would deprive them of their living as beggars! They end up standing at a place where the procession with the reliquary of Saint Martin is going by and both of them, in spite of themselves, are restored to health! There was also a mystery play, *Mystère de la vie de saint Martin*, composed in 1496 by a man named André de la Vigne, which was performed in the city of Seurre in Burgundy; the performance lasted three days; the work consisted of no less than twelve thousand verses.

This should suffice to indicate the importance of the literary work by Sulpicius Severus down through the centuries; even today it conveys to us, quite vividly, the sense of a contemporary of Martin who saw him live, who managed to penetrate the secret of his sanctity, and who felicitously communicated the admiration that it inspired in him.

Martin's Sanctity

The reader may be amazed by the great popularity of devotion to Saint Martin, but actually it is something else that ought to be surprising: the marvelous thing is that, in an age when sanctity tended to be identified with martyrdom, people recognized in Martin the traits of authentic holiness. With him the chapter on confessors of the faith began. Sulpicius Severus did not fail to state his views on this subject:

> Although the character of our times has been such as not to afford him the opportunity of martyrdom, he none the less will share the martyr's glory. If it had been given to him to have a part in those struggles that were waged in the days of Nero and Decius (I call the God of heaven and earth to witness) he would have mounted of his own free will upon the rack or he would have flung himself spontaneously into the fire.

From that time on, besides the martyrs (or, rather, after them), the Church would honor those who, like Martin, "confessed their faith" in a striking way. Thus, in his day, people would celebrate the memory of Basil of Caesarea or of Athanasius.

Based on a quick overview of Martin's life, one might agree somewhat with Saint Brice (Brictio or Britius), who declared that there was nothing extraordinary about it: nothing reminiscent of those who had endured fire and the sword, nothing reminiscent, either, of the desert Fathers who sought out solitude and distinguished themselves by battling against ferocious, terrifying demons or by their astonishing ascetical practices, such as those of the stylites a little later on. Saint Martin, on the contrary, is—we might say—an everyday saint. Above all he accepted life as it was presented to him: a soldier for as long as it was required of him; a bishop when he was elected to the office, whereas meanwhile he had done all that he could to remain in minor orders as a simple exorcist, not even daring to receive priestly ordination, convinced as he was of his unworthiness.

And perhaps that was precisely the most humble, the least visible form of holiness that he could practice. No one around him made any mistake about it: it was precisely in his daily routine that he found God. In everyday life, with its lowly duties, its little conflicts, its modest gains. How could anyone have imagined that an Absolute Being, such as the one who brought the Good News, could find a place in everyday life? During the first three centuries of the Church's life, being Christian involved making a radical break: with the surrounding society, with the common way of thinking and acting, with the authorities, with the prevailing customs; it was a matter of offering up one's life, which meant handing it over to the executioners. Martin, on the other hand, bowed to normal living conditions that were not of his own choosing. Yet from his youth, by treating his slave like a brother, he completely set himself apart from the other soldiers; day after day, his conduct refuted slavery. This was a productive patience that in him, and to the astonishment of those around him, helped destroy an institution that went back thousands of years. Allowing the absolute to penetrate the everyday, we repeat, was Martin's accomplishment. At a time when the desert Fathers, especially in the East, kept pursuing that grand combat that consisted of confronting the demon directly, Martin was humility itself, serving a slave and cleaning his shoes. It made him almost ridiculous, and he knew it; what he didn't know was that in this way he was opening up immense vistas for the most routine life.

His example was all the more important inasmuch as he was responding exactly to the needs of the times in which he lived. The entire civilization was undergoing a radical transformation: the way man or the progress of mankind would be viewed from then on had changed. It was no longer solely a question of being the conqueror, the strong man with power at his disposal, the wise man to whom nothing in the intellectual world is foreign, from philosophy to poetry—the man who, freed from the contingencies of the common people, can imagine that he is a superman and, in any case, finds himself free to choose, to develop the line of thought that suits him, be it only to deny himself anything that is excessive in his passions, as the Stoics did. The animating principle from now on, of the individual human being and furthermore of society, is the deposit of the faith, which has been received and which is destined to be handed down and lived out by means of the simplest command there could be: to love your neighbor as yourself, to love as God loves us. It is no longer a matter of rebuilding the world, even according to the laws sanctioned by this wisdom, but rather to receive everything from God. Martin strikes us neither as a humanist nor as an ideologue: he just prays.

His dealings with others, whatever sort of people they may be, are disconcerting as well. Brice might well fly into a rage against him, insult and provoke him, yet he remains silent, smiling; but all it takes is for him to notice that someone is shivering in the cold and that no one is watching, and there he goes, sharing his garment with him. To him, the other person is sacred. And this is probably the sign that faith is authentic: for someone motivated by faith, the other, whatever sort of person he may be—powerful, like an emperor, or rejected, like a beggar on the street, friend or enemy—stands for all humanity. In our days Mother Teresa changed one whole part of the world simply because one day she saw a man dying in the street, and she took him away to care for him. In his time, Martin inaugurated an entire civilization: he very humbly took the first steps toward making every Christian responsible for his neighbor.

And it really was a new civilization that he inaugurated—a civilization with profound components that were not always perceived. The people who lived then—it's only normal—were most often aware of the collapse that was taking place: the central, hierarchical authority that had become bureaucratized and militarized was now left in tatters. Less than a century after Martin's death, the last emperor was deposed. The few remaining literary men were dismayed to see the language evolving toward an irremediable break-up: the Latin language was scarcely used any more except in the Church, where the initiative of a Saint Ambrose gave rise to the development of marvelous hymns, which flouted, however, all the rules of meter and accentuation. Anyway, what significance would the learned distinctions of the poetic art have for the barbarians who had infiltrated the state and the population? This is the question posed in the fifth century by Sidonius Apollinaris: "How do you compose a verse in a six-foot meter when your patron's name is seven metrical feet long?" He said this as the Burgunds were approaching, the barbarians who would give their name to the French province of Burgundy. In their wake, Venantius Fortunatus would

complain that he had no way of making his poetry comprehensible to barbarians such as the Bavarians and the
Alamanni. When Augustine died, he was the bishop of
Hippo, and he would be the last bishop of that city. Everything seemed to crumble, even around those who, following
his example, were clinging to the City of God.

This happened in the year 430. Before Augustine, in the
year 420, Saint Jerome died, leaving to civilizations yet to
come a peerless legacy: the Bible, to which he had given new
form and expression in the common language, the Vulgate.
No one then could have suspected that, on the basis of such a
treasure, a whole new civilization would develop. The first
seeds, however, did spread and spring up in the centuries
immediately following. Now the region sown by Martin
would be the new center where the new era could mature:
the Loire region, from Tours to Poitiers, would prove to be
extremely productive in incubating the civilization that was
to come.

In this sense it is impossible to exaggerate the importance
and the influence of the life and example of Martin or the
significance of his form of sanctity. As a soldier, he was different from the other soldiers on one essential point: the respect
he had for his slave. As a bishop, he was different from the
other bishops who settled down in their town, celebrated the
liturgy in their cathedral, and taught those who were around
them. Without fanfare, without announcing his intention,
without in any way reproaching the others, he constantly
overstepped the limits of his city and of his diocese; he became the itinerant bishop, because he was concerned about
instructing the people of the countryside, the *pagani*, who
had remained pagan. He did not look for crowds, but spoke
to little groups of villagers. This is perhaps not what the
people of Tours expected when they called on him to be

the head of their diocese, but it was what would raise up the steeples of our villages and bring about the flowering of rural France.

We might add that he was not a monk like the others, either. Indeed, around him gathered the first monks of Christian Europe: not so much around a master who preached as around a man of prayer whom they wished to imitate. The rule, the canonical hours, the way of monastic life would come later on, with Saint Benedict. Nevertheless, Ligugé and Marmoutier both would serve as a sketch for the monasteries that would spring up everywhere in Europe, thanks to the person of Martin. He himself would do no more than devote himself to common prayer and hospitality toward others, giving birth to these initial groups, which were destined to have such numerous offspring.

Yet his kind of sanctity is still much less striking than that of Anthony or of Pachomius: none of that rigorous asceticism of the sort practiced by those who secluded themselves in the desert in order to live as hermits or cenobites; none of those staggering combats, either, confronting the devil or the hostile powers. Instead, a simple, frugal life—although Martin approved when his confreres caught a great big fish for Easter supper!—and a hospitality marked by simplicity and humility, the memory of which remained so vivid for Sulpicius Severus. A routine life permeated with prayer, led under the watchful eyes of the Lord.

Which does not mean that it aroused no astonishment. And there was just cause: on three occasions Martin restored to life human beings considered dead! It is difficult to go any father than that in working a miracle.

Nowadays people don't like to use the word "miracle" very much, unless it is to speak about the "miracles of science", which are all the more marvelous in that there is nothing miraculous about them, since they are generally the product of long and patient research that has been conducted in an intelligent manner, with astounding results.

Sulpicius Severus did not speak of miracles in the biography of Martin, but he often used the term in his *Dialogues*. In his time, a miracle was considered as a consequence of the faith proclaimed in the Gospel: "He who believes in me will also do the works that I do; and greater works than these will he do, because I go to the Father. Whatever you ask in my name, I will do it" (Jn 14:12–13). But clearly, someone who was seeking miracles and not faith would be mistaken.

In our time, people also have questions about the presence of the devil, which was not uncommon in the life of Martin. As we related the anecdotes we commented on possible interpretations of this negative force that was striving to turn him away from God and that, incidentally, did not always present itself in terrifying shapes, as in the visions and spiritual combats of the Eastern ascetics; didn't he once assume the appearance of Christ himself, robed in purple and crowned with a diadem? But Martin rejected him, precisely because he did not expect Christ to appear in majesty, crowned as an emperor.

In many instances, moreover, Martin seems to have imputed to the devil the anger or the stubbornness exhibited by certain individuals, beginning with Brice, his disciple. Diabolic interference is taken then as a figure of speech.

Our age might perhaps rebuke Martin for being fond of relics. He had asked Saint Ambrose of Milan for relics of the martyrs Gervase and Protase. He may even have had relics of the Theban legion, that is, of Saint Maurice (Mauritius) and his companions, who were massacred at Agaune by order of Emperor Maximian toward the end of the third century, probably in the year 286. In that narrow pass of Agaune, which could be called the "key to the Rhône valley", the soldiers of the Theban legion (who came from Thebes in Egypt) refused to carry out an order that would have required them to take up the sword against their Christian brothers; hence they were condemned to death. They were decimated, then massacred to the last man, together with their leader, Saint Maurice. Martin had every reason to be interested in their story. Another tradition has him traveling to Agaune and gathering up the blood of the martyrs that reappeared on the grass at the place where they had been massacred. But that is only a pious tradition of which there is no written record before the twelfth century; Sulpicius Severus did not mention any such pilgrimage by Martin. What is certain is that the martyrs of the Theban legion were not buried until long after the massacre, and that the first shrine in honor of them was built at the site of their collective martyrdom during Martin's own lifetime, around 360 or 370, by Theodoret, the bishop of Octodure.

It is quite plausible that, by one means or another, Martin managed to procure some relics of Saint Maurice and of his companions for the church in Tours. At the time of Gregory, his successor, they would have been the object of solemn devotions.

This veneration of relics would become more and more pronounced with the succeeding centuries. Recall, if necessary, that it corresponds to a very natural tendency: keeping reminders of a beloved person—a flower or a lock of hair—has been a custom in every age. In our day, photography has made this desire concrete and has superseded to some extent the need for an object that belonged to the person who is departed or sorely missed. From the religious standpoint, however, the custom has been maintained; every altar on which Mass is celebrated contains some relic. But this veneration of relics has in the past been the object of troubling exaggerations, which have given rise to indecent trafficking and shameless abuses. The centuries following the one in which Martin lived, at least, left a legacy of incomparable masterpieces in the form of reliquaries.

The fact remains that Martin was very much a man of his era, while also heralding the ages that would follow, in that he was concerned about the relics that would be housed in his cathedral in Tours. His own relics, as we have seen, were the object of exquisite care and veneration on the part of the faithful who later traveled there on pilgrimage—and they were also the object of savage fury in the destruction that took place in the sixteenth century and later.

Finally, anyone who attempts to delve into what constituted Martin's sanctity should be profoundly grateful to his biographer, Sulpicius Severus; his manifest wonder and astonishment at Martin's faith and contemplative fervor nevertheless reveals to us what is essential in the saint's personality. In recent years some have criticized him for that wonder. Controversies have cropped up on this subject: Is his account still credible or not? Some have denied it, precisely because they themselves took certain expressions literally. The great historian Camille Jullian, who was a specialist in that period, refuted these suspicions; furthermore, he passed stern judgment on those who refused to see in the narrative of Sulpicius Severus "the unbroken thread of human deeds woven into the supernatural fabric". He concluded the series of studies that he devoted to this text by stating that "all of these deeds bear the hallmarks of a superior man, a great leader in the City of God", and he was pleased to hail Martin as having "a very sound intellect, an upright will; he was anything but a visionary miracle-worker in a continual state of prayer or an ascetic in a perpetual battle against his body".

It is tempting, moreover, to compare the life and renown of Saint Martin with that of another personage, almost his contemporary, who also enjoyed astonishing popularity over the ages. Martin the Westerner has, indeed, a counterpart in the Eastern Church: we mean Saint Nicholas, who was also a bishop and who also, in that century in which the Church was taking shape, was destined for fame and veneration that far surpassed what a bishop might expect, even one who was very popular in his lifetime. From the historian's point of view, Nicholas did not have the same resources as Martin did; he never found a Sulpicius Severus to tell his life's story. Then, too, the historical data, strictly speaking, are rather meager in his regard. He is called Nicholas of Myra or of Bari, Myra being an episcopal see in Lycia, a province of Asia Minor. He is said to have been imprisoned during the persecutions of Diocletian, yet he died in his diocesan city in the fourth century. It was not until the end of the eleventh century, in 1087, that the corsairs of the city of Bari, in southern Italy, seized the relics in Myra and made off with them; the inhabitants, fearing a Turkish invasion, had abandoned their city and the relics in it. Curiously enough, from that moment on the fame of Saint Nicholas began to grow in an extraordinary way, to the point where he became the patron saint of Russia. His cult spread throughout the East, but he is no less venerated in the West. His deeds and his miracles, however, are recounted only in the *Golden Legend*, the work of Jacobus de Voragine, in the thirteenth century. But everyone knows the story of Saint Nicholas, who brought back to life three little children whose throats had been slit by an innkeeper in Myra who had thrown them into a barrel of brine; the song on this subject is still rather popular. The story is told also of how he saved three poor girls who were going to be sold into prostitution by placing on their windowsills three purses filled with gold, which would serve as dowries for their weddings. His tomb in Bari is said to have exuded a miraculous oil; records state that it was still flowing in the fourteenth century. This inevitably recalls the miracles worked by Martin with holy oil, when he anointed the lips or some other part of the body of a sick person whom he had been asked to heal.

Nicholas, like Martin, was chosen by the people; it is related that he attended the Council of Nicaea, and that his name was already invoked in the East at the time of John Chrysostom. His cult became extremely widespread: in the city of Rome alone more than eighty-five churches or convents are dedicated to him; in Paris he was the patron saint of lawyers. Finally, we all know how he was the one who, by a strange substitution, gave birth to Santa Claus. On December 6, Christians used to give presents to children in honor of Saint Nicholas, but little by little the figure with the long beard carrying a bulging sack full of presents was transferred to the feast that followed three weeks later and was also an occasion on which to show concern for little children.

As for the names of persons and places entrusted to the patronage of Nicholas, they are too many to be counted—the more so, given that the name Nicholas includes all sorts of derivatives, such as Colas or Klaus in German-speaking lands, not to mention the feminine derivative: Nicole or Colette. The parallel between these two bishops of the fourth century, therefore, is striking enough to be worth noting; it was a sign of the Church's development that she should be graced, both in the East and in the West, by the presence of a bishop whose glorious memory has endured through the centuries.

INDEX